CIVIL RIGHTS

THE DIARY OF THREE MINORITY WOMEN FIFTY YEARS LATER!

Corinne Patrick, Liz Ross, Sandra Mobley

AuthorHouse™
1663 Liberty Drive
Bloomington, IN 47403
www.authorhouse.com
Phone: 1-800-839-8640

© 2015 Corinne Patrick, Liz Ross, Sandra Mobley. All rights reserved.

No part of this book may be reproduced, stored in a retrieval system, or transmitted by any means without the written permission of the author.

Published by AuthorHouse 01/21/2015

ISBN: 978-1-4259-0612-2 (sc)
ISBN: 978-1-4259-0611-5 (hc)

Library of Congress Control Number: 2014918416

Any people depicted in stock imagery provided by Thinkstock are models, and such images are being used for illustrative purposes only. Certain stock imagery © Thinkstock.

This book is printed on acid-free paper.

Because of the dynamic nature of the Internet, any web addresses or links contained in this book may have changed since publication and may no longer be valid. The views expressed in this work are solely those of the author and do not necessarily reflect the views of the publisher, and the publisher hereby disclaims any responsibility for them.

Scripture quotations marked KJV are from the Holy Bible, King James Version (Authorized Version). First published in 1611. Quoted from the KJV Classic Reference Bible, Copyright © 1983 by The Zondervan Corporation.

"We hold these truths to be self-evident, that <u>all men</u> are created equal, that among these are Life, Liberty, and the pursuit of happiness." **Declaration of Independence, 1776**

"All persons shall have the same rights...to make and enforce contracts, to sue, be parties, give evidence, and to the full and equal benefit of all laws..." **Civil Rights Act of 1866**

Show me your ways, O LORD, teach me your paths;
guide me in your truth and teach me, for you are God
my Savior, and my hope is in you all day long.
Psalms 25:4-5

Prelude

The Historical Years

Segregation became common in Southern states following the end of Reconstruction in 1877. Reconstruction ended as the last Federal troops were withdrawn. Southern conservatives regained control of their state governments through fraud, violence, and intimidation.

Segregation was an attempt by white Southerners to separate the races in every sphere of life and to achieve supremacy over people of color. Segregation was often called the Jim Crow system a system that pervaded the South. Schools, restaurants, all forms of transportation—all public and most private facilities were subjected to institutional separation. Virginia was one of those Southern states that enacted Jim Crow laws, which enforced separate facilities for blacks and whites.

From the 1880s into the 1960s, a majority of American states enforced segregation through "Jim Crow" laws (so called after a black character in minstrel shows). From Delaware to California, and from North Dakota to Texas, many states (and cities, too) could impose legal punishments on people for consorting with members of another race. The most common types of laws forbade intermarriage and ordered business owners and public institutions to keep their black and white clientele separated.

> I will be glad and rejoice in your love, for you saw my affliction and knew the anguish of my soul. You have not handed me over to the enemy but have set my feet in a spacious place. Be merciful to me, O Lord, for I am in distress; my eyes grow weak with sorrow, my soul and my body with grief.
>
> *Psalms 31:7-9*

Alaska:

"The instruction of Indians in the vernacular is not only of no use to them, but is detrimental to the cause of their education and civilization, and it will not be permitted in any Indian school over which the Government has any control, or in which it has any interest whatever."

Quote: ***From Report of September 21, 1887, in House Executive Document No. 1, part 5, vol. 11, 50 Congress, 1 session, serial 2542, pp. 18–23.***

California:

"African and Indian children must attend separate schools. A separate school would be established upon the written request by the parents of ten such children. "A less number may be provided for in separate schools in any other manner."

Quote: "The History of Jim Crow," n.d., <http://jimcrowhistory.org> (27 November 2009).

Texas:

"Any white person of such county may use the county free library under the rules and regulations prescribed by the commissioners court and may be entitled to all the privileges thereof. Said court shall make proper provision for the negroes of said county to be served through a separate branch or branches of the county free library, which shall be administered by [a] custodian of the Negro race under the supervision of the county librarian."

"[The County Board of Education] shall provide schools of two kinds; those for white children and those for colored children."
Quote: http://shanaburg.com/sample-jim-crow-laws/

Virginia

This act, noting that "the preservation of the public morals, public health and public order, in the cities and towns of this commonwealth is endangered by the residence of white and colored people in close proximity to one another," authorized cities and towns that adopted the provision, to be divided into districts known as "segregation districts." City councils ordered the preparation a map showing the boundaries of all such districts, detailing the number of white persons and colored persons residing within such segregation districts. One year from the passage of the ordinances adopting the provision of this act, it was unlawful for any colored person, not then residing in a district so defined and designated as a white district, to move into and occupy as a residence any building or portion thereof in such white district. Also, it was unlawful for a white person to move into a colored district. Penalty: misdemeanor, with fine for the first week between $5 and $50, and for each succeeding day of such residence the sum of $2. Quote: "Jim Crow History," <http://jimcrowhistory.org> (27 November 2009).

Corinne Patrick, Liz Ross, Sandra Mobley

"The conductors or managers on all such railroads shall have power, and are hereby required, to assign to each white or colored passenger his or her respective car, coach or compartment. If the passenger fails to disclose his race, the conductor and managers, acting in good faith, shall be the sole judges of his race."
Quote: http://cassian.memphis.edu/history/mcaffrey/JimCrowLaws.html

"Every person... operating... any public hall, theatre, opera house, motion picture show or any place of public entertainment or public assemblage which is attended by both white and colored persons, shall separate the white race and the colored race and shall set apart and designate... certain seats therein to be occupied by white persons and a portion thereof, or certain seats therein, to be occupied by colored persons."
Quote: Kutztown centennial association. Historical committee; Deatrick, W. Wilberforce, 1853- [from old catalog] ed

> All your commands are trustworthy; help me,
> for men persecute me without cause.
> *Psalms 119:86*

1914: World War I

> God is our refuge and strength, an ever-present help in trouble. Therefore, we will not fear…
>
> *Psalms 46:1-2a*

When World War (1914-1918) began, blacks enlisted to fight for their country; however, soldiers of color were segregated, denied the opportunity to be leaders, and where subjected to racism with the armed forces.

Alaska:

In April 1925, the seventh Alaska Territorial Legislature enacted into law a measure requiring that voters in territorial elections be able to read and write the English language. In 1925, the only law passed concerning minorities related to school admission. Children of mixed blood who led a "civilized life" would be allowed to attend school with white children. No specific mention of black children was made. Public accommodations segregation was barred in 1949.

Corinne Patrick, Liz Ross, Sandra Mobley

California:

In 1925, California stated that no textbooks or other instructional materials used by public schools could reflect upon U.S. citizens because of their race, color, or creed. This state was in the forefront for liberation.

Texas:

In 1919, Texas ordered that Negroes were to use separate branches of county free libraries. In 1922 in regards to Voting Rights a Texas statute stated that "... in no event shall a Negro be eligible to participate in a Democratic party primary election held in the State of Texas...." This was overturned in 1927 by the U.S. Supreme Court in Nixon vs. Herndon. In the early 1920s, a Texas statute required racially segregated schools, and public accommodations in the area of county libraries required separate branches for Negroes to be administered by a Negro custodian. By the mid-twenties, miscegenation was declared a felony. Interracial marriages were to be nullified if the parties went to another jurisdiction where such marriages were legal and in 1926, public carriers were segregated.

Virginia:

Halifax Training School had its beginning when the county school board purchased the existing facilities from the Banister Baptist Association in 1920. Later, it became the consolidated school to serve all black children in Halifax County. In the 50s it was the state's largest rural Negro high school. In the 1920s, the school year was five months long, beginning in October.

In 1924, Mayfield Grammar School (a school for blacks) opened with grades one through seven. It was the first truly public school for blacks. Mayfield Grammar was partially destroyed by fire and space for the third and fourth grades was rented in the former Williams Normal & Industrial

Institute until repairs were made. The grammar school was eventually known as the M. H. Coleman Grammar School.

In the area of laws by the state of Virginia, there weren't many, because most of the laws concerning people of color had already been enacted.

> Do not fret because of evil men or be envious of those who do wrong; for like the grass they will soon wither, like green plants they will soon die away. Trust in the Lord and do good; dwell in the land and enjoy safe pasture.
> *Psalms 37:1-3*

1929: The Great Depression Starts People Lost Jobs

> As the deer pants for streams of water, so
> my soul pants for you, O God.
> My soul thirsts for God, for the living God. When can I go and
> meet with God? My tears have been my food day and night,
> while men say to me all day long, "Where is your God?"
>
> *Psalms 42:1-3*

In 1932, Booker T. Washington High School (a school for blacks) opened with four classrooms, a library, an office, and a multi-purpose room.

The 1935 Social Security Act: Due to the Depression, the Social Security Act established a fund for pensions and unemployment compensation, providing some long-range employment security to American workers for the first time in history.

In 1939, World War II began. When World War II began in Europe in 1939, blacks demanded better treatment than they had experienced during World War I. They demanded that black soldiers be trained in all military roles and that black civilians have equal opportunities to work in war industries at home.

Alaska:

In 1935, Alaska enacted a statute outlawing discrimination because of color at the University of Alaska.

California:

In 1929, California repealed discriminatory sections of earlier codes and provided that all children, regardless of race, should be admitted to all schools. In 1931, California outlawed racial discrimination, prohibited marriages between person of the Caucasian and Asian races, and broadened earlier miscegenation statute prohibiting marriages between whites and Malays.

Texas:

In the mid-thirties, Texas established a state tuberculosis sanitarium for people of color and directed that all public carriers separate whites and blacks.

Virginia:

In the 1930s, Virginia required segregation in every theater, movie theater, opera house, or other place of public entertainment that accepts both white and colored audiences. It also classified "Negro" as any person with Negro blood; required racially segregated schools: and enacted the following bill:

Miscegenation [Constitution]
Originally entitled "A bill to preserve the integrity of the white race," it tightened miscegenation provisions. The definition of "whiteness" was

narrowed to state "no trace whatever" of non-white blood allowed. This bill nullified interracial marriage if the parties went to another jurisdiction where such marriages were legal. For the first time Virginia prohibited marriage between whites and Asians and other non-white non-Negroes. Penalty: Felony for both parties if found guilty, punishable by confinement in the penitentiary for between one and five years.

> O Lord, do not rebuke me in your anger or discipline
> in your wrath. For your arrows have pierced me,
> and your hand has come down upon me.
>
> *Psalms 38: 1-2*

1940: The Birth of Sandra Elizabeth Ford

> Come, let us sing for joy to the Lord; let us shout aloud to the Rock of our salvation. Let us come before him with thanksgiving and extol him with music and song.
>
> *Psalms 95:1-2*

Sandra Elizabeth Ford Mobley was born on September 1, 1940 in South Boston, Virginia. She was the first child of George Francis Ford and Florence Breedlove Ford. Her two brothers were George William Ford born June 5, 1944 and Breedlove born March 1, 1948. She was raised in a segregated middle-class black neighborhood. Her father G. F. Ford was the son of an elementary schoolteacher and a brick mason and the grandson of a master carpenter and an elementary schoolteacher. Her mother's parents and grandparents were well-known black tobacco farmers. Her father was Presbyterian and mother was Baptist, so she became an active member in Mount Olive Baptist Church. Because of her ardent spirit and her love of the Christian work, she married a Baptist minister, and to this union a son was born.

Corinne Patrick, Liz Ross, Sandra Mobley

By the time Sandra was born, segregation severely restricted African Americans in South Boston, Virginia. Schools in South Boston were segregated, as well as hotels, restaurants, theaters, and public facilities. Blacks and whites were forbidden to live in the same home. African Americans in South Boston survived mostly on service jobs for the white population or for their own communities. Women worked as maids, laundresses, cooks, and midwives. As late as 1940, black workers in South Boston held jobs in the lowest categories of pay and prestige, as domestic servants, service workers, or unskilled and semiskilled laborers.

Black communities developed in the areas of neighboring downtown (Church Hill) South Boston, and Uptown South Boston. For most African Americans in South Boston in the early twentieth century, to live in the Uptown communities was to live as middle-class blacks: these communities were composed mostly of schoolteachers, a few professionals, and leaders of churches and businesses

Sandra: The Early Years

She grew up in a brick house on Jeffress Boulevard in the Uptown community. There she lived with two generations of the Ford family: her mother Florence: her father, George (Dick): and her brothers, George and Breedlove. The Ford's home was on the block of houses with neatly kept yards, with hedges, oak trees, and an elementary school that was once a high school. The street was paved. Mobley's home had electricity and plumbing.

For most African Americans in South Boston, this house and neighborhood were strikingly different from the wooden buildings, outhouse privies, and unpaved street that they knew as home. Mobley's parents bought the home together, first built as a beautiful white-framed house and later covered with bricks completed by Mobley's grandfather George Washington Ford, who was one of two black brick masons in South Boston. Mobley' father was a hardworking, religious, and handsome man and a gentleman as well. He was born in Baltimore, Maryland, and later grew up in South Boston where he was a bright student. After high school, he attended Saint Paul College in Lawrenceville, Virginia, and there he became a track star.

George (Dick) Ford did not believe in segregation, but he believed strongly that it was important for African Americans to show their high morals and good manners, which he learned at home and at Saint Paul. He believed such respectability would have a supporting effect, for if African Americans worn to be good citizen of society, they would show that stereotypes of blacks were simply false. African Americans were not lazy or unintelligent or easily attracted to crime and other forms of sinning. By being respectable, they could make it difficult for white people to have such bigoted ideas about African Americans.

George (Dick) Ford's first job was at the Norfolk, Virginia shipyard. He later returned home to work at J. P. Steven & Co. a rayon mill. He was one of the first blacks to be hired at the plant when it came to South Boston.

He married Florence Glenn Breedlove, and to that union three children were born.

Mobley's mother was a housewife – and mother, and in later years worked to supplement the family's income when children were in the upper grades of high school and in college, until her death at an early age.

Baptist and Presbyterian religions were a dominant feature of the household. Florence, Sandra, George, and Breedlove were Baptist. George (Dick) was a Presbyterian and a deacon.

George (Dick) Ford's mother was a schoolteacher, and his father (who was part Indian) was a brick mason. Florence's mother and father (who were descendant of slaves) owned a tobacco farm for many years and worked and retired from a tobacco company.

> God is our refuge and strength, an ever-present help in trouble. Therefore, we will not fear...
>
> *Psalms 46:1-2a*

Civil Rights

Sandra's thoughts, knowledge, and memories:

It was my understanding that in 1940, a large percentage of black households did not have running water. Many streets were unpaved and drained poorly, so that heavy rains left them flooded and impassable. Still a black business district developed. Virtually all African Americans belonged to a church in those times. The black community developed its own clubs, hospitals, and other institutions, including the William Normal Institute. With the exception of black-owned grocery stores, barbershops, and restaurants, businesses that catered exclusively to the black community, most jobs and money depended upon the white business of South Boston.

From all reports, by custom, an African American entered a white business or home only through the back door. African Americans often shopped in separate sections of white stores and waited for white customers to be served before they were. If a movie theater allowed African Americans, they were required to enter through a side door and to sit in the balcony. Whites commonly referred to African Americans by their first names, as if their proper names did not matter,

The police, who were virtually an all-white force, freely harassed African Americans on the street. They believed their duty was to keep African Americans in their place, apart from white.

Sandra grandparents and parents experienced it all. Surely they remembered the more hopeful experience of African Americans during Reconstruction. That recent past could have seemed only brighter. For Sandra Mobley, this was the history that preceded her. She was born into it on September 1, 1940, in the midst of World War II.

IN 1942 WORLD WAR II CONTINUES

> Hear, O Lord, my righteous plea; listen to my cry. Give ear to my prayer – it does not rise from deceitful lips. May my vindication come from you; may your eyes see what is right.
>
> *Psalms 17: 1-2*

Alaska:

During these years, Alaska citizens displayed signs indicating racial discrimination and most public facilities posted signs that read "No Indians Allowed". By 1949, citizens were entitled to full and equal public accommodations. It was unlawful to display signs indicating racial discrimination. Penalty: misdemeanor; $250, thirty days imprisonment, or both.

California:

In the mid-forties, California prohibited marriage between whites and "Negroes, mulattos, Mongolians and Malays." In 1947, California subjected U.S. servicemen and Japanese women who wanted to marry to rigorous background checks. California also barred the marriage of Japanese women to white servicemen if they were employed in undesirable occupations. The state repealed an 1866 segregation law that required separate schools for the children of Chinese, Japanese, and Mongolian parentage, and repealed miscegenation laws. Prior to repeal, interracial marriages were prohibited, but no penalties were attached to such marriages, or to interracial cohabitation, or to migration into California by interracial couples legally wed out of state.

Texas:

In 1943, the state of Texas ordered separate seating on all busses. By 1949 separate washrooms were included in directives. In 1950, separate facilities were required for white and black citizens in state parks.

Virginia:

Consolidated schooling began in 1948 in Halifax County when Booker T. Washington High School of South Boston merged with the Halifax Training School in the town of Halifax.

> I will extol the Lord at all times; his praise will always be on my lips.
> My soul will boast in the Lord; let the afflicted hear and rejoice.
> *Psalms 34:1-2*

1951: THE BIRTH OF BETTY MARIE ELLIS (ALSO KNOWN AS LIZ FROM 1978 ON)

> Delight yourself in the Lord and he will give you the desires of your heart. Commit your way to the Lord; trust in him and he will do this: He will make your righteousness shine like the dawn, the justice of your cause like the noonday sun.
>
> *Psalms 37:4-6*

Betty Marie (Liz) Ellis was born March 2, 1951, in Seattle, Washington, to Arthur Virgil Ellis (of German descent) and Anna Grace Nashalook Ellis (of Alaskan Inupiaq descent). Betty was the third daughter of eight children. Her siblings: Nancy Nashalook Bernhardt, born March 9, 1944 in Nome, Alaska; Karin Ann Ellis, born May 22, 1949 in Nome; William Arthur Ellis, born September 29, 1953 in Texas; Virgil Joe Ellis, born January 2, 1955 in Texas; Roberta Lynn Ellis, born September 10, 1957 in Texas; Billy Ray Ellis, born April 30, 1961 in Germany; and Sandra Lee Ellis, born November 14, 1964, in Kentucky. Betty was raised in the military and in rural Texas.

Arthur Virgil Ellis, Betty's father is the son of Virgil Clifton and Johnnie A. Ellis of Waco, Texas. Arthur graduated from McAllen High School. Arthur's father was an engineer who worked on the Falcon Dam and his mother worked in a bomb making facility and eventually a school cafeteria. Arthur joined the U.S. Army during World War II and was stationed in Nome, Alaska to help build the communication station.

Anna Grace Nashoalook, Betty's mother is the daughter of Joe and Ola Nashoalook, descendants of Chief Nashoalook. The federal government changed the surname during the Census (unknown date) from Nashoalook to Nashalook. The family details were provided by Aunt Mary Lou in the 1960's and from reading great Aunt Emily Ivanoff Brown's book, the Grandfather of Unalakleet, which provided genealogy information. Anna was taken by the missionaries at age five and put in the St. Mary's boarding school until she graduated from the 8th grade, then she was returned to Unalakleet. Unable to speak Inupiaq, her father, Joe, sent her to Nome to work in the Polaris Lounge. That is where she met Arthur V. Ellis.

Betty: The Early Years

Laredo, Texas, is hot. We lived near a Mexican community; not sure where. Spanish is the language of choice where we lived, especially since my playmates were of Mexican descent. My grandmother said that I spoke Spanish often when playing with other kids in the neighborhood. Most of the Spanish ejidos were developed from what I have read of the history of Laredo. I do not have any memories of any of the controversy that is evolving. All that I do know is what I feel when we go places. Children are not immune to the effects of the racial controversy. According to the *Handbook of Texas Online,* blacks and Hispanics attended segregated and inferior "colored" and "Mexican" schools. As late as the mid-1950s, the state legislature passed segregationist laws directed at blacks (and by implication to Tejanos), some dealing with education, others with residential areas and public accommodations. Governor R. Allan Shivers, who opposed the 1954 *Brown v. Board of Education* decision, went so far as to call out the Texas Rangers at Mansfield in 1956 to prevent black students from entering the public school.

Alaska was no different. There were issues between the Alaskan Native and the white community.

> Keep me safe, O God, for in you I take refuge. I said to the Lord, "You are my Lord; apart from you I have no good thing."
> *Psalms 16:1-2*

Betty's thoughts, experiences, and memories

The early 1950's are hard to remember; the earliest memory was traveling to Georgia and my mom was having a hard time dealing with the heat. My dad had a window air conditioner for the car in order to keep my mother cool. On this trip, I do recall that my dad had to buy the food and bring it out because my mom, my sister, and I were not allowed in the restaurant. It was a Whites Only restaurant. My dad, who was of German descent with blue eyes and blond hair, was allowed in the restaurant. I was too young to understand at the time; however, I understood in the 1960's. During the 1950's we moved from Georgia to Japan and back to Texas. While in school in Texas, I remember having to sit in the very back of the classroom.

History in the Making

"On December 1, 1955, Rosa Parks, a seamstress in Montgomery, Alabama, refused to give up her seat on a public bus to a white man who had boarded the bus after she did. At that time, public buses in the South were segregated, and African-Americans not only had to ride in the back of the bus, but also had to give up their seats to any white person who wanted to sit. Ms. Parks was arrested and taken to jail for refusing to give up her seat. On December 5, 1955, African-Americans in Montgomery began a boycott of the public buses led by a minister who had recently come to the Dexter Avenue Baptist Church in Montgomery, Dr. Martin Luther King, Jr. The peaceful boycott continued for 381 days during which time 90% of the African-Americans in Montgomery refused to ride the buses. At the end, the buses in Montgomery were desegregated." (Taken from http://www.usdoj.gov)

Alaska:

In 1950, the Johnson O'Malley Act is passed, which transfers administrative control of Alaska schools to the Territory. By 1955, several specialists in education were placed throughout the state in district offices in order to help teachers throughout Alaska. By the late 1950's the Bureau of Indian

Affairs issued a manual on how teachers should teach in remote areas. Alaska natives were not allowed to speak their native tongue when in school.

California:

In the mid-fifties, California allowed all citizens the right to full and equal accommodations in public places; segregation and discrimination of the state National Guard was prohibited, and it was a misdemeanor for an innkeeper or common carriers to refuse service to anyone without just cause.

Texas:

In the early 1950s, it was unlawful for person of Caucasian blood to marry person of African blood. The penalty was two to five years imprisonment. There was a statute establishing a tuberculosis hospital for blacks; public carriers were segregated in 1953; and by the mid-fifties, the city of San Antonio abolished previously required segregation of the city swimming pools and other recreational facilities. By 1958, the state mandated that no child be compelled to attend schools that are racially mixed. There was to be no desegregation unless approved by election, and the governor may close schools where troops were used on federal authority. These were the years that Betty attended schools in Killeen, Texas.

> Vindicate me, O Lord, for I have led a blameless life; I have trusted in the Lord without wavering. Test me, O Lord, and try me, examine my heart and my mind; for your love is ever before me, and I walk continually in your truth.
>
> *Psalms 26:1-3*

Virginia:

A number of years later, in 1955, the two-story building was completed. It gave black children their first official cafeteria, a gymnasium, an expansive library, a fully equipped science laboratory, and an authentic home economics class space.

The name of the high school for black children was changed in 1956. On January 15, 1956, the plant was officially dedicated as the Mary M. Bethune High School of Halifax County, renamed in honor of the famous African-American educator.

The division's secondary schools were integrated in early 1970; the Halifax County High School was reorganized as the Halifax County Senior High School serving tenth, eleventh, and twelfth-grade pupils of all races. In July 1993, the school once again became Halifax County High School, with the formation of Halifax County Middle School and the addition of the ninth grade to the high school. The present Halifax County High School plant is located on Route 129, outside the town limits of South Boston, and opened for students during the 1979-80 school year.

The Ruling: Brown vs. the Board of Education

> Delight yourself in the Lord and he will give you the desires of your heart. Commit your way to the Lord; trust in him and he will do this: He will make your righteousness shine like the dawn, the justice of your cause like the noonday sun.
> *Psalms 37:4-6*

"During the 1950s, Blacks slowly prospered alongside Whites, but they were still being denied opportunities simply on the basis of race. The fortunes of minorities would soon change again; or so it would seem.... The 1954 Supreme Court ruling in the case of Brown vs. the Board of Education of Topeka, Kansas placed a damaging blow to the hearts of many White segregationists.

"A Black family challenged the segregation policies of the Topeka school district. While living just two blocks from a local area school, Linda Brown had to travel twenty-one blocks to attend an all-Black school. The NAACP saw this as excellent opportunity to challenge the "separate but equal" segregationist policies and filed the brief on behalf of the Brown family. They would argue that the Fourteenth Amendment indicated that the policy established by the 1896 Plessy vs. Ferguson ruling was unconstitutional. Earlier battles had been won, but this was the case that would test the constitutionality of segregation. Thurgood Marshall presented the brief before the Court. When the decision came in, all nine justices voted that the policy of "separate but equal" was unconstitutional. The courts ordered immediate desegregation of public schools. Blacks, for the first time in the nation's history, would be admitted to Southern White schools-at least in theory.

"Americans were shocked by the ruling and White parents were spurred into action as White citizens councils were formed throughout the South. In 1957, members of these groups came from all over the South to stop the admittance of nine Black students to a local Little Rock High School. Arkansas Governor Orville Faubus ordered the National Guard to bar admittance of the Black students. The events that followed were broadcasts on national television and America's Southern hospitality, racism, was revealed to the world. The television cameras were rolling as White mobs threatened the Black students with physical harm as they unsuccessfully attempted to enter the doors of the school. Black Civil Rights leaders pressured President Eisenhower to send federal troops to protect the rights of the students. As several presidents before him, he told the leaders that progress on the matter must come slowly. After conferring with Governor Faubus, President Eisenhower had no choice but to act. Eisenhower urged Faubus to allow the students to enter the school. When thousands gathered to prevent the students from entering the school, Eisenhower again attempted to speak with the governor. Rather than relenting, the governor left the state on a "business trip." Eisenhower federalized the Arkansas National Guard and sent in one thousand paratroopers from the 101st Airborne Platoon to protect the nine Black students. For the first time since Reconstruction, U.S. military forces were sent to a state to assist Blacks and restore order.

"Many school districts throughout the South simply closed their doors rather integrate. The results of the Supreme Court ruling were not enacted until fourteen years later. Several state legislatures did everything they could to prevent desegregation of their schools. One tactic used by legislatures was to pass numerous laws to side step the court's decision. Each of their laws would then have to be challenged in court. Another tactic used was the passage of laws requiring disclosure of NAACP membership. Once obtained, pressure was applied to employers to fire NAACP members." (Taken from Kevin Holloway at http://home.earthlink.net/~civilrightsreport/)

Virginia:

Sandra Elizabeth Ford was in high school in South Boston, Virginia. Jim Crow laws pushed blacks to the back of buses, restricted them to living in certain neighbors, and stripped them of the ballot. Even outside of the laws, the Jim Crow culture barred blacks from certain stores, paid them less for the same work, and neglected their children's education. In Virginia, separate was never equal before 1954. (School segregation was always separate, never equal.) Teachers in South Boston taught most black students in churches and lodges because there were not enough schools for black children.

During this time, Virginia became a key battleground for civil rights, The Supreme Court ended school segregation in May 1954, in part, because Virginia was far less likely to erupt in racial violence than other Southern states. In Virginia, white kids studied for and attended college, as well as looked forward to rewarding careers. Black kids were limited in their options; they trained for trade jobs, not professional positions. From classes to materials, educational investment was unequal for black children. History stated that black high schools were often called training schools to avoid offending white officials, particularly in areas without a high school for white students.

Sandra attended Halifax Training School, which changed its name to Mary M. Bethune High School in 1956. (The school was named after a prominent black educator who was born in Mayesville, South Carolina, and was the fifteenth child of former slaves.) Recognizing the need for a well-rounded education for blacks, Mary Bethune was instrumental in founding the Daytona Library and Industrial School for Training Negro Girls, which later became Bethune-Cookman College.

Black plaintiffs were less likely to encounter violence here than in the Deep South. Besides, Virginia was closer to the NAACP headquarters in New York than other Southern states were, as well as Howard University in Washington, D.C., a black college with a law school.

Scholars credit a group of Richmond, Virginia, lawyers—Oliver Hill, Samuel Tucker, and Spottswood Robinson—with coordinating most of the Virginia lawsuits. These lawyers had graduated from Howard University, just like Thurgood Marshall, a NAACP lawyer and future Supreme Court justice. At the time, Virginia did not provide a law school for black students.

Larger and better schools have followed good roads. One-room schools have become fewer, as buses carry the children to consolidated schools. Teachers are better trained too, because now there are state colleges for the training of teachers. Virginia State College in Ettrick, near Petersburg, founded for the training of Negro teachers, continues to grow to meet the needs of the ever-increasing student body. This college now has a division in Norfolk. Hampton Institute founded after the War Between the States, serves a large number of African-American students. Other universities and colleges in Virginia that give to the state a well-recognized place in higher education are Virginia Union University in Richmond and St Paul College in Lawrence. Many of these black institutions were well known far beyond the borders of the state.

> *Sandra: "The U.S. Supreme Court's landmark May 17, 1954, decision in the case of Brown vs. the Board of Education dramatically changed the history of Virginia and the nation. I learned of the decision on the evening of May 17, on a radio broadcast fifty years ago. I was at home with my parents eating dinner. At the time, I was in the eighth grade at the segregated Halifax County High School."*

THE RULING: THE CIVIL RIGHTS ACT OF 1957

> My steps have held to your paths; my feet have not slipped.
>
> *Psalms 17:5*

"In 1957, Congress enacted the first civil rights law since the period following the Civil War. The Civil Rights Act of 1957 created the authority for establishing a civil rights office at the Department of Justice. On December 9, 1957, Attorney General Herbert Brownell issued the order establishing the Civil Rights Division, headed by an Assistant Attorney General, to enforce all Federal statutes affecting civil rights, to investigate complaints of civil rights violations, to coordinate the enforcement of civil rights throughout the Department of Justice, and to consult with and assist other federal agencies in civil rights enforcement.

"In 1957, Congress passed federal civil rights laws providing for some voting rights enforcement and criminal civil rights violations prohibited by laws passed in the 1870s. The Division was very small-fewer than 10 lawyers. This handful of lawyers immediately began to investigate voting rights violations in the South.

"As time went on, more civil rights acts were passed expanding the rights that the Division's lawyers would enforce. In 2002, the Division has more than 350 lawyers dedicated to the enforcement of civil rights laws." *Taken from the Civil Rights Web site. http://www.usdoj.gov/kidspage/crt/crtmenu.htm*

Alaska:

In 1950, the Johnson O'Malley Act is passed, which transfers administrative control of Alaska schools to the Territory. By 1955, several specialists in education were placed throughout the state in district offices in order to help teachers throughout Alaska. By the late 1950's the Bureau of Indian Affairs issued a manual on how teachers should teach in remote areas. Alaska natives were not allowed to speak their native tongue when in school.

Virginia:

When Congress enacted The Civil Rights Act of 1957 I was 17 years old, a junior in high school. It was a good age to understand the meaning of The Civil Rights Act of 1957 (a voting rights bill). In 1958, I became eligible to vote. I had to take a voter qualification literary test before I could register and be eligible to vote. I can visualize the test today. When I took the qualification test, I was determined to pass on the first try. I knew I could read and write and I proved that ability. Many blacks became disqualified from voting because they could not read and write.

1961: The Birth of Corinne Angela Deborah Binning

> The Lord is my light and my salvation – whom shall I fear? The Lord is the stronghold of my life – of whom shall I be afraid?
>
> *Psalms 27:1*

Corinne Angela Deborah Binning was born September 8, 1961 in Georgetown, Guyana, South America, to David Windebank (of Portuguese descent) and Deanna Binning (of Amerindian, English, and Afro-Guyanese [Trinidad] descent).

Manly Binning was my grandfather. Manly Binning's grandfather, Robert Binning, was born in Barbados where he attended the 1745 Codrington College {the oldest Theological College in the Western Hemisphere} and obtained his Masters. Robert Binning was the owner of a printing press. Robert Binning married Lucy Spencer, the daughter of Nancy Allicock.

Manly V H L Binning was born July 15th 1899 at Wiriburisiri Canalli upper Demerara River and grew up in the Demerara River vicinity. He helped his father George Alexander Binning who was at that time owner of a Timber Grant along the Demerara River. Manly at the age of seventeen attended Queens College School for boys in Georgetown.

Manly Binning is remembered as a great father by his children. He was a brilliant coworker and mentor to the many workers of the bauxite industry in Upper Demerara, Guyana and to all his extended family one of the most important relative that ever lived. Manly was born with many exceptional talents. He was intelligent, creative, imaginative, skillful, ambitious, and very hardworking. Manly stood out as a leader among his peers and is remembered for all his great qualities.

The importance of Manly Binning to his family heritage is sacred. He was one of the few to document and record the lives of his family. He travelled by boat, train or bus to visit relatives where he conducted interviews and recorded by writing down their information and family history. He documented, organized his work, and then protected it for the future generations that can now benefit from this precious information of family heritage. He understood quite well the tangle web and interrelationships of heritage. He realized that to fully understand his linage, he had to first document the many families in the area. He recorded not only his direct linage but preserved others as well. He wrote on the families of Spencer, Allicock, DeNieuwerkerk, Hill, Mansfield, Bremner, Fiedtkou, Van Cooten, Paterson, Blount, Binning and others as he decipher and understood the family linage. His exceptional vision is reflected in his work which is why he is so dearly remembered by his love ones.

Manly Binning was married on June 22nd 1933 to Gloria Millicent Smith and had 10 children: Rex, Wilma, Barbara, Norma, Elizabeth, Jacqueline, Verna, Regina, Deanna, and George. Later, after his wife died, he wedded Eslyn Davidson and had three more children: Colleen, Manly (Junior), and Alana, who were born in his late 70s, a testimony to his superb health. Fishing was one of Manly's hobbies along with the making speed boats.

His first boat was Flash, and that boat was unlike the modern speed boats of today. It was long and slender and slid through the smooth Demerara River like a knife through butter. His next boat was Jet. The last boat that he made, Vamp, was a much shorter boat than the first two. The last years of his career with Demba,

He was an Engineer by trade. He worked for Sprostons1 at Wismar, the Steam Locomotive at Demba, then at the Power House. He continued his career at the Demba Machine Shop where he became a foreman and reported to the Chief Engineer. He spent many years in that position. During his time at Demba, Manly was a very adventurous man, and, always with a unique idea, he converted "Big Bertha," an old Steam Engine to a Pile Driver and proudly named it "Lord Manly." There were many other innovations on the job, which were contributed by Manly's ingenuity. Some of his innovations earned him commendations from the chief executive officer of Demba.

He always seemed to have answers for problems concerning his field of work, and, of course, his household. He built his own washing machine, and designed and constructed a horse-racing machine and a merry-go-round for his family's enjoyment. There wasn't a machine made that he couldn't fix. He dabbled in the other sciences of life, also. He followed a daily exercise regimen that included yoga and, even had a cure for in-grown toenails.

Manly V H L Binning was assigned to work with young men training in various trades at the Demba Trade School. After retirement in 1963, he donated his time to help out with the exams at the Trade School.

Deanna Binning-Peterson, Manly Binning's last daughter from his first wife Gloria has continued where her father has left off. Deanna is Corinne's mother. She has the same burning passion for love of family and heritage. She represents him so well. She is hardworking, thorough, kind and possessed very important knowledge on the substance of family and heritage. Her father must be smiling proudly to see that Deanna has done so well and continued his legacy.

The Demerara Bauxite Company Limited, known as DEMBA, a subsidiary of the Aluminum Company of Canada Limited 3 Arvida road is now called Republic Avenue. Arvida road was named after Alcan's Alumina smelter located in Arvida, Quebec, Canada.

Manly Binning worked for Sprostons 1897 Wismar to Rockstone Railway located at Wismar http://guyanathenandnow.wordpress.com/2011/11/06/the-demerara-essequibo-railway-der/

Corinne: The Early Years

My sister, Patricia and I lived with my grandparents until my mother came back to Guyana from the United States to take us to live in the United States. My stepfather, Herbert Arch Mitchell was a white male, age fifty-two, an American. He had moved to Guyana in 1966 with my stepbrother Herbie, whose mother had died at age two. My mother was twenty-four years old, with three children, when they got married in 1968. My step-father went to Guyana because his job sent him there to work in construction. My mother was viewed as "an island girl" due to her brown complexion.

Sandra's thoughts, experiences, and memories

In 1966, Sandra graduated from Virginia State College, Petersburg, Virginia.

In 1966, Sandra was employed at the segregated black Campbell County High School as a business education teacher.

Civil Rights

In February 1967, she married Rev. Gataroy Mobley Jr., a Baptist minister, in a ceremony wedding at Mount Olive Baptist Church.

June 1967, Florence Glenn Breedlove Ford died, and was buried in a segregated black cemetery.

April 1968 Kevin Glenn Mobley was born.

1968 Employed at the segregated black Mary M. Bethune High School.

1969 Mary M. Bethune High School changed its name to Halifax County Junior High School.

Following integration in 1969, the school became the Halifax County Junior High School and served the entire county school population until the 1979-80 school year. What was the Mary M. Bethune High School and now holds the majority of the county's public offices, the Bethune Complex began as the Halifax Normal Institute.

Betty's thoughts, experiences, and memories

During the early 1960's Betty's family were stationed in Germany. There were times when Betty was not welcome in other children's home. An early memory is a young girl in her 4th grade class that was having a birthday party and the young girl invited her to the party. I remember overhearing the child's mother scolding the young girl in the kitchen because she did not want me there. I often felt ostracized and could not figure out why I was different. During those years in elementary school in Germany, the best year was in 5th grade; this was because of my teacher Mrs. Perry, an African-American woman. She always encouraged me.

After leaving Germany, we returned to Eddy, Texas where I attended the public school system of Bruceville-Eddy, Texas. This was a public school and everybody was nice. My 6th grade teacher made me feel special; her name was Mrs. Behnke. Mrs. Behnke was always praising me for my good manners.

An early memory during this time was a trip to Waco, Texas with my grandparents to go shopping at the J.C. Penney. I had to use the bathroom; there were two bathrooms. One bathroom was marked as "Women White" and the other was marked as "Women Colored." I went to the colored bathroom because I thought that the sinks and toilets were colored. They were not. It did not dawn on me that all of the ladies in the bathroom were Negro's. Shortly after that incident, we got our housing at Fort Knox, Kentucky. The Army base was safe.

Attending a military school was good; the only differentiating factors were officers' kids and non-commissioned officer's kids. I still had issues with ethnicity. An American Indian boy from Arizona would torment me at the bus stop when I was in 9th grade; thankfully a senior by the name of Bob Risner always stood up for me. I am grateful to this day for his compassion. Kids can be cruel.

While in the 10th grade, I tried out for cheerleading and made the team. I still suffered from self-esteem issues and attribute my position due to my sister being a Varsity Cheerleader. My cheerleading coach mentioned to me that I seemed self-conscious around others and wanted to know if there is anything she could do. Of course, I kept quiet. Another girl on the squad told others in school that the coach said that I was self-centered! Boy I wish that were true. A Japanese-African-American Varsity Cheerleader berated me for this revelation. I could not wait to leave. We did, that year. I had a brief stint at Valley High School until we moved to Colorado.

I attended Fountain-Fort Carson High School for one year, my junior year of high school. I was a cheerleader, enjoyed my classes, and my teachers. I still had low self-esteem. Although the environment was not impacted as much as on the army base, there still was a sense that there were differences based on color. My dad received orders for Vietnam and we moved off post to a new area in Colorado Springs. I attended Billy Mitchell High School and did not participate in anything. Following graduation from high school, I discovered that I was not eligible for any Bureau of Indian Affairs (BIA) educational grant funds because I was not considered a Native American. These were personal turbulent times for me, growing up in a large family with alcoholic parents, my dad in Vietnam, and being responsible for my five younger brothers and sisters. My mother left the family and the Red Cross sent for my dad to be returned home.

> *Liz state: "I remember that feeling of disbelief. I lived all my life knowing that I was an Alaska native, yet I had not realized that we were not part of the BIA. What a blow to my plans to apply for a BIA grant; I was left lost."*

1970s

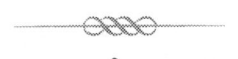

> Cast your burden upon the Lord and He shall sustain you: He shall never suffer the righteous to be moved.
>
> *Psalms 55:22*

Sandra's thoughts, experiences, and memories

The 1970's were called the cutback management era, particularly in the government field. In 1974, with a bachelor degree, I accepted employment with an agency of Virginia where cutbacks were the key factor in employment, management, and salaries. I had my share of experiences from the time I was hired until I retired.

While working in my state government agency, I earned two degrees – a master's degree and a doctor's degree - with no financial support from my agency or state government. My manager told me that I was not qualified for reimbursement or educational assistance from my employment and he/she would not sign for me because my degrees were not related to my employment. My manager emphasized that an MBA and a DPA were not needed for my kind or job. Not only did I apply within my agency, but throughout the Commonwealth. I applied for an advanced position more than one can imagine. It was stated to me that it is not what you know, but whom you know. I experienced age discrimination, education discrimination, and salary discrimination!

Betty's thoughts, experiences, and memories

As a young adult, I finished high school after my dad returned from Vietnam. We were living in Colorado Springs, Colorado. I had a low self-esteem and figured that college was out of the question since we had no money for higher education. My dad encouraged me to take typing, shorthand, and bookkeeping in my senior year of high school. This was the best thing I ever did. Those skills will prove helpful in life.

I moved to Fort Sill, Oklahoma in the early 1970's and married Dennis C. Williams, a Captain in the U.S. Army. The marriage did not last. I returned to Colorado Springs, Colorado. During this time I worked for Colorado Springs Equipment Company and waitressed for Prange's Restaurant until I married Blant Norris Reeves, III. I moved to Maryland during this marriage and began college at Harford Community College.

I enjoyed being at Harford Community College (HCC). I participated on the Tennis Team and the Bowling Team, and People to People. As an older student, it was not bad. I was serious about school and learning. My final term at HCC, I was in Honors English. I wrote a short story about my mother and Alaska. I still have that hand-typed story.

Being an Alaskan Native was considered special. Everybody wanted to know about Alaska and he/she always said that Alaska was on a wish list to visit. This was a good time for me and helped boost my self-esteem. While at Harford Community College, I was in Honors English and wrote a short story about my mother and Alaska life. The professor told me that

I should have it published. I never published the story. I became separated from my husband during this time.

I was excited to know that the Bureau of Indian Affairs were seeking applicants for fellowship grants from Alaskan Natives. I applied and hand-carried my papers to Washington, DC. I was so excited, especially since I had a 3.92 GPA. I received the fellowship grant plus an additional scholarship (Elizabeth Brownley Memorial Scholarship). By 1976 I graduated and was accepted into Loyola College in Baltimore, Maryland; however, at the last minute I changed my mind and switched to the University of West Florida in Pensacola.

While attending the University of West Florida, I worked as a temporary administrative person for the construction company building the West Florida Hospital. It was there that I experienced the issue of race when a worker asked me what reservation school I attended. The construction company was originally from Alabama and it was apparent that this particular individual was not very knowledgeable about Native Americans and, in particular, Alaskan Natives. I made up some name like Waxachie Native Reservation and he said that it must have been a good Indian school because I sounded so smart. Wow.

I began working at Digital Systems of Florida in 1978. During this time, I meet Jeffrey S. Ross, whom I married and remain married today. While at Digital Systems, racial disparity was not an issue but gender was an issue. It was during this time that Betty changed her name to Liz.

Corinne Patrick, Liz Ross, Sandra Mobley

Corinne's thoughts, experiences, and memories:

As a child, I came to the United States on September 24th 1970. I am of mixed race. I came from Guyana, South America. I had just turned nine years old; I was thinking that coming to America was the most exciting thing that anyone could experience. This was the land of opportunity. I would no longer have to go to bed with hunger pangs. I would no longer have to wear shoes with holes, and the best part I would have my own bed without my cousins, aunts, or sister.

We were a blended family before a blended family exists. The first place that we lived was Carson, California. I was the only brown, complexioned child in the class: all the children were white. I can remember coming home disturbed because the children would pull my ponytail and ask me, "Why is your hair so curly? Are you a nigger? It was disturbing at first, I would go in the bathroom and cry without letting any-one see me. But after a while I began to fight back, and this caused many problems for me later on as I grew up.

After we left Carson, we then moved to Covina California and I did whatever it took to be accepted in the white group. I had my mother put a straightening perm in my hair so my hair would not be frizzy; I also had her hot comb my hair in order for my hair not to frizzy. This tactic continued on for six years (1970-1975), I faced the issues of an all-white schools, and in an all-white community.

My best friend, Laura, lived across the street and she was a year younger than I. I played baseball, football, ran track, but the best was basketball. I was taller than most of the kids in the neighborhood and could play basketball. During that time, they called me Kareem-Abdul Jabbar, because I could play ball. In 1975, I went to the unemployment office to apply for a job and was asked about my ethnicity and for what I was qualified I was only fourteen years old, and only qualified for babysitting and cleaning. I therefore I started cleaning an elderly women's home.

In my high school years, I attended a multi-racial high school in Oxnard, was accepted in the black community, and ran track for four years. I dated African-Americas. My step-father disapproved of this; he stated that he did not believe in inter-racial dating. We moved to Oceanside, where my step-father insisted that we attend Vista High School where the majority were whites: however, I found myself again blending with blacks because I was accepted in the culture.

1980S TO THE MID-1990'S

> Teach me, O Lord, to follow your decrees; then I will keep them to the end. Give me understanding, and I will keep your law and obey it with all my heart.
>
> *Psalms 119:33-34*

Sandra's thoughts, experiences, and memories:

Getting a promotion in state agencies has been a pain. My earned BS, MBA, and DPA degrees meant nothing to my agency. To feel good about myself, I decided to join professional organizations so that I could utilize my knowledge and skills. I became a top leader as president, vice president, chair, or co-chair in most of my professional organizations with good followers. I also attended many professional conferences as a presenter, a representative, and regular attendee. The good relationships I had outside of my job offset the bitterness I received in my state employment.

Liz's thoughts, experiences, and memories:

In the 1980's I was busy building a family and ensuring that this marriage to Jeffrey S. Ross works. I was committed to this effort. Christopher was born in May of 1980; I was having problems at work at Digital Systems of

Corinne Patrick, Liz Ross, Sandra Mobley

Florida. I became pregnant immediately and Mark was born May of 1981. It was during this time that I left Digital Systems because of controversy with a woman who accused me of sending a letter to her husband stating that she was having an affair with the owner of the company. I never knew about this letter until after I delivered my second child; it turned out that another woman in the department sent the letter. I suppose that it was more convenient for someone to state it was me. I was hurt that I was accused of something I did not do. She never apologized. I have learned that women can be more lethal than men in the workplace.

In 1983 we decided to move to Maine to be closer to Jeff's family and for better job opportunities. We had a garage sell to sell off some of our items before embarking on the trip up to Maine. It was during this time that I experience an issue with race. A woman wanted to purchase a chair we had and she spoke to me as if I could not understand English. She used her hand movement to write a check and spoke slowly and loudly stating that the check is just like money, etc. I was dumbfounded and kept quiet. Jeff immediately came up to talk to the woman, afraid that I was going to do something. Anyway, I fumed about that.

During the 1980's my mother was more in touch with her family. One thing my mom never did was talk about her life or her family. Occasionally she will say something in passing like how the nuns would beat her when she spoke Inupiaq with other kids. Or, how she was taught to make bread while at St. Mary's and she became responsible for baking bread each day.

In 1982, I attended Federal Income Tax and Corporate Tax Training at the University of Maryland as part of my training with Ernst & Whinney. While at the training, a young lady from the Anchorage, Alaska office was in attendance. I approached her and told her that my family was originally from there. She immediately shunned me and avoided me whenever I was

Civil Rights

around. I was taken aback; however, given that during that time there was an increase in alcoholism with Natives, it was easy to label me the same.

In 1983, I was transferred to the Portland, Maine office of Ernst & Whinney. We moved from Sanford, Maine to Derry, New Hampshire. Christopher and Mark seemed to adjust well with the moves. Jeff had been working with a former partner from his business in Bangor, Maine before our Digital System days. Life was good.

I worked part-time as a direct sales person for home décor and holiday gift company. This proved to be lucrative. The first year I earned a trip to Greece and the year after I earned a trip to Rio De Janeiro. After that I started working with a personal care company in direct sales. This was fun as well and I earned a trip to San Francisco.

In December 1984, Kathryn Leigh was born. Finally, we had a girl to add to our family of boys. We moved into a larger home in Londonderry, New Hampshire. After the move, I did some free-lance consulting work for a couple that was finishing up a healthy eating book. It was not long before we were in the home in Londonderry that I became pregnant with Kevin. During the 1980's, I was consumed with the family.

After Kevin was born, I returned to martial arts training. I began working for House of the Samurai as the Program Director. I spent six days per week at work. My husband, Jeff and the kids trained with me.

Corinne's thoughts, experiences, and memories:

I worked at a fast-food restaurant for three years starting at age sixteen. Once I graduated from high school I worked at Burroughs Corporation for eighteen months on the assembly line until I went into the U.S. Army in February 1981. I received Christ as my personal Savior in November 1981 while station in Germany.

I was married in July 1982 to Michael Patrick Sr. from Georgia, an African-American. We had meet in the army in 1981, while stationed in Germany. We currently have four children: Kamlyn born in 1983: Monica, born in 1987: Miriam, born in 1992: and Michael Jr., born in 1994. All four were born while we were in the military.

The military was a good move for me: I stayed in for fifteen years, until January 1996. During my first eight years of military service, President Regan was in office, and therefore I received several pay raises, including 12 percent increase in 1982. While in the Army I had many challenges: In 1982 I received my promotion to PFC E-3. However, the platoon sergeant wanted sexual favors in exchange for a promotion to the next promotion grade. I informed him I would stay a private till I got out rather than exchange sexual favors for a promotion.

In 1984, we were brief from one of the first female sergeant major, she informed the audience that if we wanted to be promoted in "this man's army" we must have a different focus, and that family was not a number-one priority. For this cause she had decided not married or have any children. At the time, I had one child, and thought to myself, "Well, I guess I won't be promoted in this man's army!"

In 1984, I went to the E-5 Sergeant Board for promotion to a noncommissioned officer. After the first promotion, I accelerated rather quickly: however, the points were high in my field and I had to meet challenges in order to be promoted. This is the reason that I went to college in 1985: to be promoted to the next rank. I received my AA degree in 1987 from Chicago City Colleges while stationed in Garlstedt, Germany.

I was promoted to E5 in 1986, and then went to the E6 Board in 1987 while I was pregnant with my second child. However, at that time I was six months pregnant, and it was considered a high risk pregnancy. Once, at the board for promotion, the sergeant major approached me concerning my weight issue since I had gained a lot of weight during the pregnancy. Needless to say, I did not pass. My blood pressure was elevated and I was so upset they put me on bed rest for the rest of my pregnancy. I went into the field in August in 1988, and I injured my back and was Med-Evac to the emergency room after falling off the back of a two-and-a-half-ton truck. I went back to the E6 Board in 1988, and passed with flying colors, lost seventy-five pounds after the pregnancy, and was promoted to E6 in August 1989.

I went to Germany in November 1989, and then was deployed in December 1990 as part of Desert Shield/Storm. During this time, I had two children: eight years old and three years old. They both had to go to my mother's home in Vista, California while both of us were deployed in Desert Storm. We were attached to the First Armored Division, but we were part of the Third Infantry Division stationed in Aschaffenburg. Not knowing the status of our return, we entrusted God to ensure that our children would be well taken care of. We returned from the Gulf in June of 1991, and I flew to California to pick up my two girls.

Upon returning from the Gulf, we went to Fort. Irwin, California, where I made the decision that I did not want to compromise my family and go to a war zone and risk my children being raised by another person. Once I went to Fort Irwin, I had two more children, Miriam in 1992, and Michael in 1994. I therefore prepared myself to get out of the military by attending college; my first priority was to get my bachelor's degree. California Baptist College had a sixteen-month degree program if you already had an associate's degree. I attended and graduated in June 1994, and then went into the master's program that was offered at Golden Gate University, Fort Irwin, which was a thirteen-month program, and graduated with my MPA in August 1995. I was pregnant while going to school and serving active duty. I was driven to complete these degrees because I wanted to position myself in case I planned on getting out of the military.

In June 1995, my husband took the early retirement that was offered to the military to those that had fifteen-plus years in. The government had made a decision to down size the military and offer early retirement. He had made the decision to retire, and I would stay until…. Later that year, I came down on assignment to go back to Germany. This time I would be assigned to a unit that was going to Bosnia. My husband and I made a decision that I would get out on a medical discharged after almost fifteen years of service.

In January of 1996, I was discharged from the military due to a medical condition with my back; I was not fit for duty. During the years since I injured my back, I have faced many challenges. We moved to Houston, Texas, in 1996.

> Know that the Lord is God. It is He who made us, and we are His; we are His people, the sheep of His pasture.
>
> *Psalms 100:3*

Corporate America - Challenges in the Late 1990s

---⚬⚬⚬---

> I call with all my heart; answer me, O Lord,
> and I will obey your decrees.
>
> *Psalms 119:145*

Sandra's thoughts, experiences, and memories:

My experiences have been in local, state, and federal government agencies, nonprofit government agency, and in education (middle, high school and universities). The challenges I experienced were in leadership positions as professor, teacher, finance director, and administrator in public and non-profit businesses or community organizations.

Outside of my state government workplace, the 1990's were great. The main highlight was receiving my MBA degree in 1998. A dream I thought I could use in my workplace, but never did. I received no bonus, no increase in salary, no promotion and no reimbursement for the cost of my MBA degree. After I received the degree, I announced my achievement at a departmental meeting. My manager was totally surprised. He did not realize my potential as an employee. Because of my investment in state government, I did not apply for jobs in corporate world, since many corporate businesses were downsizing in the 90's.

Liz's thoughts, experiences, and memories:

The late 1990's were good, for the most part. I was heavily involved volunteering with the 13th Regional Corporation and worked full time at the House of the Samurai. The 13th was experiencing unusual growth but there were some questionable activities with one of the members of the board in the area of a business. With my full time job, I was on a quota with a base pay and bonus. Every time I met a quota, my contract was changed with a different pay amount. It was getting difficult to maintain a moving target. I started working for the New Hampshire State University System and this helped in the area of health benefits for the family.

While working for the university system, I completed my Bachelor's degree. During this time; however, I was having problems with the advisor and campus director. I got out of work at 6:30 pm, which meant that the 6pm class was already in session. I contacted the instructor before the start of the term to get permission to arrive late due to my work schedule. The instructor was accommodating; however, the advisor and director met with me and said that I could not show up late for class because it sets a bad example to others in class for the college. I contacted the Human Resources Department about this situation and they agreed that it was the course instructor's discretion and not a work mandate. This led to tension in the office. I eventually sought another job.

I began working in direct sales with Avon Products as a District Manager. The job had one caveat to it; the district was to be downsized due to the changing strategy by the company. This did not bother me and the job turned out to be a blessing. Not only did I receive an automobile, I worked around going to graduate school full time. I was able to finish my MBA in two semesters with New Hampshire College (now called Southern

New Hampshire University). After the downsizing of the Avon District and my graduation with an MBA, I started working part-time with New Hampshire College as an Academic Advisor. While as an advisor and with the encouragement of two previous graduate instructors, I applied to Nova Southeastern University to work on a doctorate.

Corinne's thoughts, experiences, and memories:

It took nine months before I would get a job; I ended up working on the assembly line at Compaq Corporation. During my orientation I talked with the instructor and informed him of my degree, and he then passed my information on to the agency which called me and I then started working as a contractor as a purchasing assistant. I did that for nine months. I applied for several positions before and during working, and one of the biggest issues that I was faced with was I was over-qualified and did not have enough experience in the industry. Military experience had no weight because it was a different industry. I started working for a 3PL in June of 1997 as an operation supervisor, and later was faced with many challenges as a minority female in corporate America. I had too much education, not enough experience, and was not an aggressive team player. I was later offered another position as a purchasing supervisor, but I did not fit in the mold of an operations supervisor. I did not participate in after-hours activities. I did not play golf. Nothing documented; however, the unspoken said quite a bit. I did research on projects while others took the glory/credit. I operated money making projects and generated revenue for the organization, but bonuses were weighted the same as the norm.

> Your statutes are wonderful; therefore I obey them. The unfolding of your words gives light; it gives understanding to the simple.
>
> *Psalms 119:129-130*

Nova Southeastern University Years

> Teach me knowledge and good judgment,
> for I believe in your commands.
>
> *Psalms 119:66*

Sandra's thoughts, experiences, and memories:

In September 1999, I enrolled in the doctoral program at NOVA Southeastern University in Public Administration. Working on my doctorate was not a secret to my employer or within the agency because my annual leaves were used to attend classes. Luckily I had enough leaves to complete my advanced education. I completed my doctoral course work and the writing of my dissertation in two years and four months. I graduated in 2002. I requested in writing to my manager for reimbursement for a portion of my tuition, but was told it was not job related and was refused the request.

Liz's thoughts, experiences, and memories:

In March 1999, I was accepted into Nova Southeastern University's (NSU) doctoral program. My husband was probably more excited and perhaps nervous, for me. Nevertheless, he was always my strong support system. During this time, I began adjunct teaching undergraduate finance and business classes part-time.

My first class was May 1999 in Brattleboro, Vermont. I was both excited and extremely nervous. I pulled into the parking lot of the class location at the same time as a woman that I thought was the instructor. I rolled my window down and asked, "Are you the instructor for the Nova Southeastern class?" The woman vehemently said, "No, I am a new student." That was my first meeting with Corinne Patrick. Since that day, we have been close friends. I always figure that it was ordained by God.

During that first class with Nova, Corinne and I mapped out our classes so that we could be together and encourage each other. We doubled up our classes and finished our course work within a year, sat for the comprehensive exams around the same time (different terms), worked on our dissertation simultaneously, and graduated together in 2002!

Work during this time was somewhat different. At the end of 2000, while an adjunct instructor, I was approached to apply for an interim campus director position for Franklin Pierce College. I did and I was hired. It was then that having higher education became a problem with a male colleague. This male colleague was a campus director in Concord and did not have a Master's degree (but was finishing his degree in 2001). It seemed that everything I did he would complain (he had family ties to the main campus) and it was becoming more difficult to work. Thankfully, the contract was an annual contract and not something long-term. This proved to be a blessing as well because my husband and I planned on moving to Florida. The year I graduated from NSU, I worked part-time as a recruiter for NSU and was hired full time with the Florida Partnership for School Readiness.

Civil Rights

Corinne's thoughts, experiences, and memories:

In May 1999, I was accepted into the doctoral program at Nova Southeastern University. My employer was surprised that I had been accepted, and did not realize I had a master's degree. To his surprise, I have finished and completed my doctorate. I was criticized by many for still working in the organization and having the degree. I had applied for several positions while in the company and have received several reasons for denial: too much education, pay scale (they would not be able to pay me what I was worth), lack of experience, etc...

> Your word, O Lord, is eternal; it stands firm in the heavens.
> Your faithfulness continues through all generations;
> you established the earth, and it endures. Your laws
> endure to this day, for all things serve you.
> *Psalms 119:89-91*

STATE TIMELINE HISTORY

> The Lord is my shepherd, I lack nothing. He makes me lie down in green pastures, he leads me beside quite waters, he refreshes my soul. He guides me along the right paths for his name's sake. I will fear no evil, for you are with me; your rod and your staff, they comfort me.
>
> *Psalms 23:1-4*

Alaska Timeline history: The following works were valuable sources in the compilation of this timeline: History Timeline of the Alaska Indians http://nativeamericanencyclopedia.com/history-timeline-the-alaska-indians/; Alaska Public Lands Information Centers: Timeline of Alaska http://alaskacenters.gov/alaska-timeline.cfm; Timeline of Alaska History http://www.rootsweb.ancestry.com/~akbridil/Timeline.htm; and Native News http://www.nativenews.net/nnn_history2010.shtml.

1579: Sir Francis Drake's Secret Voyage to Northwest America brought him to Alaska's southeast (Chatham Strait, south of Juneau, between Baranof Island and Kulu Island).

1725: Peter the Great dies and Empress Catherine becomes head of Russia. Vitus Bering explored Northwest coast; established Russia's claim.

1728: Vitus Bering first sighted St. Lawrence Island and one of the Diomede Islands and went ashore.

1741: June 4 - Vitus Bering on the St. Peter and Alexei Chirikov on the St. Paul set sail from Kamchatka, Siberia. On June 20 they lose sight of each other in a storm and continue on their separate voyages.

July 15 - Aleksei Chirikov along with the Danish Explorer, Vitus Bering, sights the Aleutian Islands. Chirikov, in command of the ship the St. Paul, sighted what is believed to be Prince of Wales Island of the Alexander Archipelago. Chirikov sights land and drops the anchor of the St. Paul. After losing two crews sent to shore to explore, he continues on to Unalaska and probably the island of Adak. He also loses some of his crew to disease and scurvy, before returning to Kamchatka. Bering's ship, the St. Peter, had sailed a more northerly direction and came upon Kayak Island the next day

July 18 - Vitus Bering sights Mount St. Elias in North America. He and his men were shipwrecked on Avacha Island off Kamchatka and many died of disease and lack of food.

December 8 - Bering dies on the island of Avacha and is buried there. The island is later renamed Bering Island.

1745: Russian fur traders first sight Attu and land there to trade with the natives. Several natives were killed.

1784: The first white Russian settlement embarked upon Kodiak, Alaska.

1788: The Russians enslave Aleuts to hunt fur seals.

1799: Czar Paul claimed Alaska as Russian land; he became the first Russian governor of Alaska.

1865: Western Union Telegraph Company prepares to put telegraph line across Alaska and Siberia. Last shot of the Civil War fired in Alaskan waters

1867: The United States purchased Alaska from Russia. Russia sold 375 million acres to United States for $7.2 million (about 2 cents per acre).

1877: First mission school for natives is founded.

1887: English is required in Indian Schools.

1906: Homesteads were allotted to the Alaskan Natives.

1912: Alaska became a Territory.

1920's: "Signs were placed, prior to that time, on business establishments saying... "No Indians allowed"... or... "We cater to white trade only"... and some went so far as saying... "No Indians or dogs allowed here." Quote from Roy Peratrovich to the Editor of the Anchorage Daily News, December 10, 1971. Retrieved from http://www.alaskool.org/PROJECTS/ANCSA/ARTICLES/ADN/Close_Look_at_ANB.htm

1922: Alaska Agricultural College & School of Mines, later the University of Alaska, opens at College near Fairbanks. When it opened in 1922, the Alaska Agricultural College and School of Mines had six students, one building, and an annual budget of $30,000. It became the University of Alaska in 1935 and has since added campuses at Anchorage and Juneau.

1924: Alaska Citizen Act was passed giving Alaska Natives citizenship without losing their tribal rights or property.

1925: Alaska law required voters to be able to read and write English.

1926: Ben Benson created the Alaska Flag.

1936: Congress extends the Indian Reorganization Act to Alaska. Nell Scott of Seldovia becomes the first woman elected to the Territorial Legislature.

1942: Aleut men, women, children, and elders forced to live in internment camps.

1945: Governor Gruening signed Anti-Discrimination Bill.

1946: Boarding school for Native high school students opens at Mt. Edgecumbe. Universal Services was formed in 1946 to provide catering and other support services for the civilian workforce rebuilding defense bases in Alaska.

1959: Alaska becomes the 49th State of the United States. William Egan becomes Alaska's first governor. The Alaska Statehood Act includes provisions to not take lands of the Native people.

1st organized efforts began in the 1960's when the U.S. Atomic Energy Commission was planning to set off a nuclear device at Cape Thompson known as Project Chariot. Residents of Point Hope, Kavalina, and Noatak, worried about the potential danger of radioactive contamination to themselves and to the animals which they hunted for their livelihood.

The threat to native land rights during the 1960's came because of the Alaska Statehood Act. The Native Allotment Act allowed a person to obtain title to 160 acres of land if he could demonstrate use and occupancy over a five-year period. The BLM rejected hunting and fishing activities as proof of use and occupancy under the act. Hence the reason only 101 allotments had been made in Alaska since the Act was adopted.

It would be a full decade before the Alaska Native Claims Settlement Act would be passed by President Nixon (December 18, 1971). ANCSA provided 40 million acres of land and compensation of $962.5 million. There would be 12 regional corporations established to administer the settlement. All U.S. citizens with ¼ or more Alaska Indian, Eskimo, or Aleut blood who were living when the settlement bill was enacted were qualified to participate, unless they were member s of the Annette Island Reserve community of Metlakatla (they had been granted a reserve by Congress in 1891, following their emigration from Canada).

Why corporations? The theme of the 1971 AFN convention was "In the white man's society, we need white man's tools." Therefore, under ANCSA, all money and all of the land goes initially to business corporations. It was through the corporations that all of the benefits flow to enrolled Natives.

Section 7 of ANCSA covered Regional Corporations.

7(i) Seventy percent of all revenues received by each Regional Corporation from the timber resources and subsurface estate shall be divided annually by the Regional Corporations among all twelve Regional Corporations. The provisions of this subsections shall not apply to the thirteenth Regional Corporation.

7(j) During the first five years following the enactment of the Act, not less than 10% of all corporate funds received by each of the twelve Regional Corporations shall be distributed among the stockholders of the twelve Regional Corporations. Not less than 45% of the funds from such sources during the first five-year period, and 50% thereafter, shall be distributed among the Village corporations in the region and the class of stockholders who are not residents of those villages. In the case of the thirteenth Regional Corporation, if organized, not less than 50% of all corporate funds received under section 6 of ANCSA shall be distributed to stockholders.

1971: Betty Ivanoff Menard (Betty's cousin) becomes the first Alaskan Native woman to summit Denali (known as Mt. McKinley).

1975: Work began on the Alaskan oil pipeline. The trans-Alaska pipeline would be completed after three years of work.

1976: The "Molly Hootch" Case was settled with a commitment by the state to provide local schools for Alaska Native communities.

1980: President Jimmy Carter signs the Alaska National Interest Lands Conservation Act (ANILCA).

California Timeline history: The following works were valuable sources in the compilation of this timeline: Seeking El Dorado: African Americans in California (edited by Lawrence B. De Graaf, Kevin Mulroy and Quintard Taylor), California's Black Pioneers: A Brief Historical Survey (by Kenneth B. Goode) and the website of the California Legislative Black Caucus. http://bancroft.berkeley.edu/reference/africanamerican/timelines.html

The Spanish Era (1769-1821)

September 28, 1542 Juan Rodríguez Cabrillo's ship entered San Diego Bay, which marked the discovery of Alta California.

1765: The Inspector General of New Spain, José de Galvez, began to develop plans for the further expansion, exploitation, and colonization of Alta California.

1781: 26 of the first 46 settlers of Los Angeles were black or mulatto.

1785: Blacks and mulattos made up at least 19.3 % of the population of Santa Barbara.

1790: Blacks and mulattos constituted nearly 15% of the total San Francisco population and 18.5% of the settlers in Monterey. The population of Baja California included 844 Spanish-speaking persons of whom 183 were mulattos.

1793: Francisco Reyes, a mulatto settler, was elected to serve as mayor of Los Angeles.

The Mexican Era (1821-1848)

February 1821: Mexico declared its independence from Spain. The Republic of Mexico was established on November 19, 1823.

1826: Peter Ranne, a black man, was a part of the first overland party to California, led by Jedediah Smith.

January 31, 1831: Emanuel Victoria, a mulatto known as "The Black Governor", took the oath of office as political and military governor of California.

1841: Black merchant William Alexander Leidesdorff, a native West Indian, settled in California where he operated a trading vessel between San Francisco Bay and Hawaii. In 1846 he purchased several parcels of property located in what is now the heart of San Francisco's financial district and eventually built San Francisco's first hotel.

1843-1845: Jacob Dodson, a free black, was in the Fremont expeditions to California. Another free black, Saunders Jackson, joined Fremont's fourth California expedition in 1848.

1845: Leidesdorff was appointed American vice consul at Yerba Buena Cove and authored the official report of the Bear Flag incident. Pio Pico, a mulatto, became Governor, an office he held until leaving California in exile after the 1846 capture of Sonoma by the United States. James Beckwourth, a famous African American hunter and scout, took part in the Bear Flag rebellion. He later served as a U.S. Army scout and carried mail between Monterey and southern California.

January 13, 1847: The Treaty of Cahuenga, ending the U.S.-Mexican War in that area, was signed by Andres Pico (brother of Pio Pico) and Major John C. Fremont.

February 2, 1848: The U.S.-Mexican War formally ended with the signing of the Treaty of Guadalupe Hidalgo. Under the treaty the United States acquired all of Alta California, New Mexico and Texas.

September 1, 1849: The California Constitutional Convention began. Of the forty-eight delegates elected to the convention, seven native Californians participated including the mulatto Antonio Maria Pico, former prefect, mayor, and legislator of San Jose.

November 13, 1849: The California Constitution was ratified almost unanimously by the white male voters in the territory.

The United States Era (1850- present)

September 9, 1850: California was admitted into the United States as a free state.

1851: An extensive body of discriminatory legislation was erected in California including the testimony restriction which outlawed testimony by African Americans, Chinese, and Native Americans against whites in court.

1862: Sensing growing white support at the beginning of the Civil War, San Francisco African Americans formed the Franchise League to campaign for voting rights and an end to the testimony restriction.

1863: The increasingly Republican California legislature removed discriminatory barriers in education and repealed the testimony restriction of 1851.

1866: After campaigning for better schools throughout the Civil War, African Americans gained access to California public schools with the proviso that separate schools could be established along racial lines. Campaigns against this stipulation continued because small numbers of African Americans within larger white communities often made separate schools financially unfeasible.

1868: San Francisco businesswoman and former slave, Mary E. Pleasant sued a local streetcar company after a driver refused to allow her aboard. Although she initially received a $500 judgment, the ruling was eventually overturned by the California Supreme Court.

1875: While most California communities had admitted African American students into integrated schools by this time, schools in San Francisco ended segregation officially in 1875.

1893: The California State Assembly passed an anti-discrimination statute prohibiting segregation on streetcars.

1903: The Southern Pacific Railroad brought in almost 2,000 African American laborers to break a strike by Mexican American construction workers, effectively doubling the African American population in Los Angeles and sparking lasting interracial tension.

1913: The first California branch of NAACP was established in Los Angeles.

1918: Attorney Frederick Roberts, a founder of the civil rights organization Forum, was the first African American to be elected to the California Assembly.

1941: Reverend Clayton Russell formed the Negro Victory Committee in Los Angeles, a group of public officials, professionals, union leaders, and NAACP members, working for the creation of jobs in defense plants for blacks.

1942: Jobs in California defense industries opened to African Americans after labor shortages, African American organization protests, and pressure from the Fair Employee Practices Commission.

1943: While aimed primarily at the Mexican American population of Los Angeles, local police arrested more than 100 African Americans in the mob violence stemming from racial tension known as the "Zoot Suit riots".

1944: The Western Regional Office of the NAACP was established in San Francisco.

1953: The U.S. Supreme Court declared the enforcement of residential race-restrictive covenants illegal in Barrows v. Jackson. Race-restrictive covenants were long utilized in California to racially segregate residential areas. Los Angeles NAACP attorney Loren Miller was part of the legal team that lobbied the Supreme Court.

1954: In the landmark case Brown v. Board of Education the U.S. Supreme Court ruled that separate schools for black and white children were unconstitutional. David Blackwell was the first African American appointed full Professor at the University of California, Berkeley.

1959: The California legislature passed the Fair Employment Practices Act, establishing a statewide Fair Employment Practices Commission to protect the people of California from discrimination in employment. Former vice president of the Brotherhood of Sleeping Car Porters, C.L. Dellums, was appointed to California's first Fair Employment Practices Commission. He served on the Commission for 26 years.

1962: After serving for 28 years in the California State Assembly, Democrat Augustus Hawkins became the first African American Congressman from California when he was elected to the U.S. House of Representatives.

1964: Proposition 14 reversed fair housing measures by California state and local governments. The proposition was sponsored by the California Real Estate Association after the 1963 California legislature passed the Rumford Act prohibiting racial discrimination in the sale or rental of certain state housing. The NAACP challenged Proposition 14 and its appeal succeeded in the California and U.S. Supreme Courts in 1967. The American Civil Liberties Union filed a suit against the Los Angeles City Board of Education regarding de facto school segregation. Subsequently, the California Supreme Court ruled that Pasadena's segregated school system was unconstitutional.

September 1, 1964: Joshua R. Rose was appointed as the first African American to serve on the Oakland City Council. He was voted into office in 1965 and served until his retirement in 1977.

1965: Five days after President Johnson signed the Voting Rights Act of 1965, there was an uprising in the largely African American community of Watts, which lasted 6 days and left 34 dead and 1,000 injured.

1966: Huey Newton and Bobby Seale founded the Black Panther Party in Oakland. Mervyn Dymally, a Los Angeles teacher and political field coordinator, became the first African American to serve in the State Senate. (In 1974 he was elected as Lieutenant Governor and in 1980 he ran for Congress representing South Los Angeles County. He became the first foreign-born black to serve in the United States Congress.) Los Angeles attorney Yvonne Brathwhaite Burke became the first African American woman to hold office in the California Legislature and in 1972 became the first African American woman elected to the U.S. Congress from California.

1968: The City of Berkeley school board inaugurated the nation's first non-court-ordered busing plan. Berkeley's plan instituted comprehensive two-way elementary school busing for the purpose of desegregating the school system and the program remained in effect for more than 25 years. In its peak year of garnering support, the Peace and Freedom Party chose Black Panther leader Eldridge Cleaver as its candidate for the President of the United States. Cleaver carried almost 37,000 votes.

1969: The city of Compton elected California's first African American mayor, Douglas Dollarhide. The newly established Black Studies Department begins operation at the University of California, Berkeley.

1970: Ron Dellums was elected to the United States House of Representatives by a largely working class district in Oakland. He remained in office until his retirement in 1998.

Spring 1971: The Afro-American Studies Department at the University of California, Berkeley graduated its first class of students majoring in the discipline

1973: Tom Bradley was elected mayor of Los Angeles, the first African-American mayor of a major U.S. city. Bradley went on to serve five terms.

Civil Rights

1977: Wiley W. Manuel was the first African American to be appointed to the California Supreme Court. He served until 1981.

1978: In Bakke v the Regents of the University of California, the U.S. Supreme Court declared racial quotas unconstitutional. However, it supported the basic principals of affirmative action in higher education. Barbara Christian became the first African-American woman to win tenure at the University of California, Berkeley.

1992: Four Los Angeles Police Department officers were acquitted of accusations that they had beaten African American motorist Rodney King. The verdict heightened racial tensions and sparked violence in Los Angeles.

1996: California Proposition 209, which banned the use of racial preferences in admissions decisions, was passed.

2003: California Proposition 54, which proposed a ban on the classification of any individual by race, ethnicity, color or national origin in the operation of public education, public contracting or public employment, was defeated.

Texas Timeline history: The following works were valuable sources in the compilation of this timeline: Texas History Timeline from e-ReferenceDesk, Lone Star Junction, and from the Texas State Historical Association, http://www.texasalmanac.com/topics/history/timeline-texas-history.

1598: A thanksgiving ceremony is held near present-day El Paso by Juan de Onate, the members of the expedition, and natives of the region. Franciscan missionaries celebrate mass, the Spaniards provide game, and the local Indians supply fish.

1685: Texas claimed by the French explorer René-Robert Cavelier, Sieur de La Salle (1643-1687) for France

Corinne Patrick, Liz Ross, Sandra Mobley

1700's: Spain establishes Catholic missions throughout Texas

1820's: Racial attitudes that supported segregation of African Americans probably arrived in Texas during the 1820s in company with the "peculiar institution," slavery.

1835: Anglo-Americans began extending segregation to Mexican Americans after the Texas Revolution as a social custom.

1836: The siege of the Alamo by Mexican troops led by Santa Anna.

1850's: Texas gives up claim to land that includes more than half of what is no New Mexico, about a third of Colorado, a corner of Kansas, the Oklahoma Panhandle, and a small portion of Wyoming in exchange for the United States' assumption of $10 million in debt.

1865: June 19 slaves were freed. War veterans returned angry.

1876: A new constitution segregated schools and a poll tax was established to support the segregated groups. This is seen as a control mechanism. For minority groups, segregation existed in schools, churches, residential districts, and most public places such as restaurants, theaters, and barber shops.

1889: The Democratic Party created "white-only pre-primary elections." (NOTE: See 1953 where the U.S. Supreme Court ruling.)

1890's: Although the law specified equal access to common school funds, black schools often did not have equal access.

Late 1800's: Institutionalized segregation flourished legally in places with a visible black population and was extended informally to Tejanos. Most Texas towns and cities had a "Negro quarter" and a "Mexican quarter."

Early 1900's: Black and Mexican schools faced lamentable conditions endemic in an antiquated educational system, and educational reforms of the era did not improve matters.

1901: The Texas legislature passed a poll tax as a requirement for voting. Given the economic difficulties of the times, the poll tax caused participation by African Americans, poor whites, and Mexican Americans to drop sharply.

In 1910 and 1911: The Texas Legislature passed laws dictating that railroad companies provide separate waiting rooms in railroad stations for whites. Several towns throughout Texas adopted residential segregation laws. The adoption of laws continued through the 1920's.

1920's: Black schoolchildren were more likely to miss school than white students, black teachers received less pay and training than their white counterparts, and teaching accommodations ordinarily amounted to one-room buildings generally under the tutelage of a single teacher. The same circumstances applied to Hispanic students, who were segregated because some whites thought them "dirty" and because some white employers desired an uneducated, inexpensive labor pool. Whatever schools existed often suffered from inadequate financing, poor educational facilities, and racist curriculum. Shunned by white society, minorities formed their own PTAs and school organizations.

In the case of the black campuses, their own sports and academic rivalries were formed. Parallel clubs and athletic teams were not as common in Mexican schools since Mexicans were considered "white" and thus did not receive the budgeting African Americans did from the "separate but equal" policy. These educational inequalities persisted into the 1950s.

1923: The Supreme Court ruled that white primaries established by political parties were unconstitutional.

1927: The Texas state legislature passed a bill that authorized political parties to establish their internal practices. This led to the Democratic Party reinstating the white primary.

Late 1920's: Numerous towns throughout Texas had segregation laws. Laws called for segregated water fountains and restrooms.

1930's: Black citizens could not attend sports or cultural events, eat at the better restaurants, or get lodging at the finer hotels unless these facilities provided separate accommodations. None of these laws specifically had Mexicans in mind, but white society nevertheless generally excluded them. Often, Mexican Americans could not commingle with whites at barbershops, restaurants, funeral homes, churches, juries, theaters, or numerous other public places.

In the workplace, minorities similarly confronted segregation. Numerous craft unions, for example, refused membership to black and Tejano workers, and unions founded by African or Mexican Americans were ordinarily segregated. Generally, blacks and Mexicans received less pay for doing the same job as whites. Separationist practices led blacks to seek employment in such menial roles as gardeners, cooks, bootblacks, and maids. Mexicans turned to fieldwork or other types of unskilled tasks such as construction and railroad maintenance in urban areas.

1944: Another Supreme Court case ruled that it was the white primary was unconstitutional.

After 1944: The National Association for the Advancement of Color People (NAACP) and other organizations worked to register black voters. Regardless of the efforts, major disfranchisement continued.

Civil Rights

1950: After the United States Supreme Court case Sweatt v. Painter mandated that the University of Texas law school admit black students, several undergraduate colleges in Texas took the cue and integrated their own campuses.

1954: The Supreme Court decision in *Brown v. Board of Education* declared the unconstitutionality of the "separate but equal" doctrine in schools, public vehicles, eating establishments, and the like. Mexican Americans won their own protracted struggle in a series of favorable verdicts from Texas courts that weakened racial separation.

1948: Delgado v. Bastrop ISD verdict prohibited school boards from designating specific buildings in a school campus for Mexican children.

1953: In a US Supreme Court ruling (Terry v. Adams), it was declared that the white-only primary is unconstitutional.

1954: The U.S. Supreme Court in Hernandez v. State of Texas declared Mexican Americans to be a class to whom Jim Crow laws could not be applied.

1956: Many white Texans did not accede easily to federal mandates or to some of their implications. The voters approved a referendum that opposed compulsory attendance in integrated schools and another that prohibited intermarriage.

1957: The Texas legislature passed laws encouraging school districts to resist federally ordered integration, though Governor Price Daniel ignored such laws in the late 1950s.

1964: Legal segregation passed into history.

Sandra Ford Mobley's Timeline and Other Information

1940 Sandra Elizabeth Ford Mobley was born in South Boston, Virginia

1944 George William Ford (Sandra Mobley's brother) was born in South Boston, Virginia.

1946 Sandra Ford Mobley attended the William Normal Institute, in grades one and two.

1948 Sandra Ford Mobley attended the Booker T. Washington-Matthew Coleman Elementary School

1948 Breedlove Ford (Sandra Mobley's brother) was born in South Boston, Virginia

1953 Sandra Ford Mobley graduated from segregated Washington-Coleman Elementary School.

1953 Sandra Ford Mobley attended the Halifax Training School, a segregated high school.

1958 Sandra Ford Mobley graduated from Mary M. Bethune High School, Halifax, Virginia.

1958 Sandra Ford Mobley became of legal age to vote.

1958 Sandra Ford Mobley attended a segregated college, Virginia State College, Petersburg, Virginia.

1966 Sandra Ford Mobley graduated from Virginia State College, Petersburg, Virginia.

1966 Sandra Ford Mobley was employed at the segregated black Campbell County High School as a business education teacher in Rustburg, Virginia

1966 Sandra Ford Mobley received Virginia Teaching Licensure Certificate from Virginia State Board of Education, Richmond, Virginia

1967 Sandra Ford Mobley married Rev. Gataroy Mobley, Jr., a Baptist minister, in a ceremony wedding at Mount Olive Baptist Church, South Boston, Virginia

1967 Sandra's mother, Florence Glenn Breedlove Ford, died and was buried in a segregated black cemetery in South Boston, Virginia

1968 Kevin Glenn Mobley was born to Rev. Gataroy and Sandra Mobley.

1968 Sandra was employed at the black segregated Mary M. Bethune High School, Halifax, Virginia

1970 Sandra, a co-founder, helped to organize The Adventuretts Club, South Boston, Virginia

1970 Sandra was a member and secretary of Halifax/South Boston, Virginia PTA Board

1970 Sandra was a director/planner of wedding activities in South Boston, Virginia

1970 Sandra was a church organist for several churches in South Boston, Virginia

1970 Sandra completed the requirements for Library Science at University of Virginia, Charlottesville, Virginia

1974 Sandra was employed at the Pittsylvania County Community Action Agency, Chatham, Virginia

1975 Sandra was a chartered member and correspondence secretary for National Chapter Mary M. Bethune Alumni & Associates in Halifax, Virginia

1976 Sandra was a chartered member and the first president of Halifax Chapter Mary M. Bethune Alumni & Associates

1977 Sandra wrote the Accounting Manual for Pittsylvania County Community Action Agency, Chatham, Virginia

1979 Sandra was employed with the Commonwealth of Virginia.

1979 Sandra wrote the Accounting Manual for CETA at Virginia Employment Commission, Richmond, Virginia

1980 Sandra enrolled in courses at J. S. Reynolds Community College in Computer Technology

1985 Sandra was the first president of the organized Richmond Chapter of the Mary M. Bethune High School Alumni & Associates – The Chapter has raised over $10,000 for Scholarship Fund

1991 Sandra was a math tutor in the adults GED Program in Henrico, County Virginia

1992 Sandra was a math tutor to at-risk students for an after school program in Richmond, Virginia

1994 Sandra attended training in Customer Service in the Public Sector at Virginia Employment Commission, Richmond, Virginia

1995 Sandra attended training in The Essentials of Credibility, Composure and Confidence at Virginia Employment Commission in Richmond, Virginia

1995 Sandra joined National Association for Female Executive

1997 Sandra attended Toastmasters International Public Speaking for college credit at Averett University

1997 Sandra joined the Phi Theta Kappa International Honor Society

1997 Sandra joined the American Business Women's Association

1998 Sandra received a MBA from Averett University, Danville, Virginia

1998 Sandra prepared a successful marketing plan for Breedlove's Fish Market.

1998 Sandra completed a research on "The Impact of the Americans with Disabilities Act on Deaf and Hard of Hearing Americans in the Workplace" for her Master's Thesis

1998 Sandra completed an annual report called "Highlights" for the Richmond Chapter Virginia State University Alumni Association

1998 Sandra was the president of the Richmond Chapter Virginia State University Alumni Association. Initiated the Chapter to raise over $10,000 for VSU first Endowed Scholarship Fund

1999 Sandra attended a Grantsmanship Workshop at Virginia Commonwealth University, Richmond, Virginia

1999 Sandra attended a Workforce Investment Act (WIA) Videotape Program at Virginia Employment Commission, Richmond, Virginia

1999 Sandra composed a newspaper called "The Lions" for the Richmond Chapter Mary M. Bethune School Alumni and Associates

1999 Sandra completed a proposal entitled "Mobley and Mobley Services (MMS) for Deaf and Hard of Hearing Adults

2000 Sandra received the Chapter President of the Year Award given by Virginia State University Alumni Association

2002 Sandra received her Doctor of Public Administration (DPA) Degree from the H. Wayne Huizenga School of Business and Entrepreneurship of Nova Southeastern University, Ft. Lauderdale, Florida

2002 Sandra presented a Conference Paper "Decision-making on Alternative Placements and Structures for Improving Adult Education Programs in Virginia," Virginia Association for Adult and Continuing Education, Charlottesville, Virginia, April 2002.

2003 Sandra's father, George Francis Ford, died and was buried in South Boston, Virginia

2003 Sandra initiated into Pi Alpha Alpha Honor Society the National Honor Society for Public Affairs and Administration

2003 Sandra selected for membership in Sigma Beta Delta International Honor Society in Business, Management, and Administration

2003 Adjunct Professor: Central Michigan University, Department of Public Administration

2003 Book Review - Journal - Public Manager - "Attack on the Federal Government Workplace--Views from Within." - Author: Oman, Ray C. "Attack on the Federal Government Workplace--View from Within." International Journal of Public Administration, 2003 - p. 26. http://www.amazon.com/Attack-Federal-Government-Workplace-Views-Within/dp/B000ALOG3G

2003 Sandra presented a Conference Paper "Decision-making on Alternative Placements and Structures for Improving Adult Education Programs in Virginia," American Society for Public Administration 64th National Conference, Washington, D.C., March 2003.

2003 Sandra presented a Conference Paper "Restructure of the Office of Adult Education and Literacy in Order to Strengthen the Quality of Adult Basic Education Programs in Virginia, Hampton, Virginia, February 2003.

2004 Sandra was inducted into the Alpha Kappa Alpha Sorority, Inc. Tau Phi Omega Chapter

2004 Sandra was initiation into Pi Lambda Theta International Honor society and professional Association in Education Virginia Area Chapter

2004 Adjunct Professor - Online: American International University, Department of Business Administration 2004 Sandra's Book Review - "Attach on the Federal Government Workplace—Views from Within" by Ray C. Oman. The Virginia Report (April 2004): 2. http://www.thepublicmanager.org/resources/bookReviews.aspx

2004 Sandra presented a Conference Paper "Ethics, Economics, & Productivity: Considerations in Public Administration Practices," Conference of Minority Public Administration 33rd Annual National Conference, Tulsa, Oklahoma, March 2004.

2005 Adjunct Professor - Online: American Military University/American Public University, Department of Public Administration – Public Safety, National and Homeland Security

2005 Sandra's Invited Lectureship "Decision Making in Government: The Wallace S. Sayre Model," Virginia State University, Petersburg, Virginia

2005 Sandra presented a Conference Paper "Diversity-Driven School Design: Decision-Making on Alternative Placements and Structures for Improving Adult Education Programs," Pi Lambda Theta 2005 International Leadership Conference, New Orleans, Louisiana, July 2005.

2005 Sandra presented a Conference Paper "Making Partnerships Work: Strategies for Success," National Forum for Black Public Administrators, Richmond, Virginia, April 2005.

2005 Sandra presented a Conference Paper "Civil Rights: The Impact of Minority Issues and Women," National Forum for Black Public Administrators, Richmond, Virginia, April 2005.

2005 Sandra was vice president of Alpha Kappa Alpha Sorority, Inc. Tau Phi Omega Chapter

2006 Sandra accepted to be on the Doctoral Dissertation Advising Committee - Research Grants: Pi Lambda Theta International Honor Society and Professional Association in Education

2006 Sandra's Invited Lectureship "Alternative Placement in Adult Education," Virginia Department of Education Conference, Charlottesville, Virginia,

2006 Sandra received the Medallion Award in Education from Mary M. Bethune High School Alumni & Associates in South Boston, Virginia

2007 Sandra was president of Alpha Kappa Alpha Sorority Inc. Tau Phi Omega Chapter

2007 Sandra is the founder of Step to Success Toastmaster International Club, chartered in June 23, 2007 in Henrico, Virginia http://steptosuccesstoastmasters.toastmastersclubs.org/history.html

2007 Sandra received Distinguished Toastmasters Medallion Awards from Toastmasters International

2007 Sandra was inducted into the Toastmasters International Hall of Fame in Roanoke, Virginia

2007 Sandra presented a Conference Paper "Delegate to Empower," Toastmasters International District 66, Richmond, Virginia, February 2007.

2008 Sandra presented a Conference Paper "Unsung Hero," Petersburg National Pan Hellenic Council, Petersburg, Virginia, June 2008.

2008 Sandra was the first president of the Richmond East End Public Library Advisory Board, Richmond, Virginia

2009 Sandra a member of American Society for Public Administration

2009 Sandra a member of Conference of Minority Public Administrators (COMPA)

2009 Sandra a member of Section for Women in Public Administration (SWPA)

2009 Sandra presented a Conference Paper "Generational Gap in the Classroom," E-learn Workshop, November 2009.

2009 Sandra presented a Conference Paper "A Shinning Star" (A Master's Roast Speech) Toastmasters International District 66 Conference, Richmond, Virginia, November 2009

2009 Sandra was vice president of Pi Lambda Theta International Honor Services and Professional Association in Education Virginia Area Chapter

2010 Sandra presented a Conference Paper "Leadership and Ethics in Public Administration," Midwest Political Science Association, Chicago, Illinois, April 2010.

2010 Sandra was appointed president of the Virginia Group for the Dorothy L. Height Endowed Scholarship Fund, Virginia Union University, Richmond, Virginia. The Group raised over $15,000.

2010 Sandra Co-Chaired the Virginia State University Alumni Fountain Scholarship Fund and the group raised over $125,000

2010 Sandra joined the Treble Clef and Book Lovers' Club, Richmond, Virginia

2011 Sandra presented a Conference Paper "Our Historical Challenge for Government and Public Sector Administrators," 34th Annual Conference on Teaching Public Administration, Williamsburg, Virginia, May 2011.

2011 Sandra presented a Conference Paper "The Decision Making," Troy Public Administration Conference, Williamsburg, Virginia, May 2011. Panel 14 Mobley Slides.pdf - Teaching Public... www.teachingpa.org/.../2011/2011slides/Panel%2014%20 Mobley%20Sli...

2011 Sandra presented a Conference Paper "Four Steps to Know Persons Completely," Toastmasters International Presenter, Richmond, Virginia, November 2011 Outstanding Mother of the Year given by the National Sorority of Phi Delta Kappa, Inc, Alpha Zeta Chapter

2011 Sandra was elected to the National Board of the Virginia State University Alumni Association, Officer – Chaplain

2011 Sandra joined the Richmond-Henrico Retired Teachers Association

2011 – 2014

My superior academic achievement signals a commitment to excellence and the beginning of a journey of lifelong learning.

Throughout my career, I have maintained positive relations with my communities. I have been successful in organizing and implementing several successful major fund-raising events. The fund raisings were for general scholarships, church building accessories, and scholarship endowment fund. All of the fund raising expectations were exceeded.

Planning, managing and supervising events for up to 1,000 people have been a challenge. Participants have come from different states in the United States and abroad. With the help of dedicated colleagues, all events were highly successful.

The non-profit organizations under by leadership have paid tribute to public service individuals who have exhibited high standard of excellence and dedication in the community. These organizations have provided recognitions to outstanding college bound students, conducted public programs on topic of community interests, provided volunteered services to non-profit organizations in health and educational arenas, provided mentors and role models for youths and young adults, contributed to academic and career developments though recruiting campaigns and scholarships, and established support team with other organizations.

All of the organizations that I have been a founder and co-founder are successfully operating financially. One of the main purposes of each organization is to give scholarships to eligible students who plan to pursuit an education beyond high school. Another purpose is for members in the organizations to have the opportunity to build confidence, build good communication, think strategically, and rely on their experience and wisdom. These attributes are important to a successful leader.

My greatest professional accomplishment in employment was the opportunity to be a university professor. I thank the AIU, APUS, and Central Michigan University who gave me the opportunity.

I have had a blessed life with the help of the Lord and Jesus Christ. My parents, siblings, grandparents, marriage, son, education, friends, acquaintances, and extended relatives have played a part in the success of my life. They were great supporters. Psalm 27:1 The LORD is my light and my salvation; whom shall I fear? The LORD is the strength of my life; of whom shall I be afraid?

Praise ye the Lord

SUMMARY

QUOTES:

BACK THEN: Black kids went to all-black schools and whites went to all-white schools because the government told them to.

TODAY: Schools still are largely segregated by race because our housing and social patterns are segregated by race.

CONCLUSION: You can have as much integration as you want in schools and neighborhoods, as long as you can afford it.

BACK THEN: State-sanctioned segregation divided students by race into separate all-white and all-black schools.

TODAY: Academic "tracking" in integrated schools, divides students into classes that end up largely divided by race. Whites and Asians go to "gifted and talented programs," blacks and Latinos go to "special education."

CONCLUSIONS: It is not enough to put students of different races in the same buildings. We also need to close gaps in achievement.

BACK THEN: White segregationists helped white parents avoid integration by sending their children to all-white private academies.

Civil Rights

TODAY: White conservatives help black parents avoid poorly performing public schools in Milwaukee, Cleveland and Washington, D.C. with vouchers to send their children to mostly-black private schools.

CONCLUSION: You don't have to be a segregationist to end up with a segregated situation.

BACK THEN: Thanks to dedicated teachers and parents, a lot of black graduates of under-funded segregated all-black schools managed to go to fine universities and succeed professionally.

NOW: High-stakes testing actually may be preventing youngsters from having a chance to prove themselves in college.

CONCLUSION: The law of unintended consequences resurfaces: sometimes the remedy for a bad situation creates victims of its own.

BACK THEN: In the early 1950s, more than 80 percent of black children were born to married parents. The percentages of black and white babies born out of wedlock were about the same.

TODAY: Only 31 percent of black children are born to married parents, compared to about 74 percent of white children. Paradoxically, as the wage rate for black workers has gone up, so has our out-of-wedlock birth rate.

CONCLUSION: While we celebrate civil rights advances we need to strengthen one of our biggest engines of success: the black family.

BACK THEN: "We believed (the Brown decision) was going to transform the world," says James F. Cone, a prominent black theologian.

TODAY: Dr. Cone observes that the Brown ruling "reminds Americans of the gap between what is and what ought to be."

CONCLUSION: Brown has helped to transform American, but we still have a lot more work to dol.

BACK THEN: Legal action spearheaded by Thurgood Marshall and the NAACP Legal Defense Fund changed the law from an obstacle into an advantage for African-Americans in their pursuit of civil rights and equal opportunity. It also spurred a decade of civil rights protests: back lash, legislation, and ultimately grand reforms.

TODAY: We have narrowed the gap between black and white income and achievement, but, unfortunately, we have widened the gap between black haves and have-nots.

CONCLUSION: We need a new black liberation movement that the courts alone cannot provide. We need to work with our families, schools, churches and other institutions to take full advantage of the hard-earned victories that have come over the past half-century.

The past sixty years have given me optimism about the progress African-Americans can make, once they are given the opportunity. Our next big challenge is to narrow the achievement gaps for those who have been left behind.

Let us hope it does not take another sixty years for us to do it.

1956

In the fall of 1956, the General Assembly held a joint public hearing to consider whether to change Virginia's constitution to permit public funds to be used to pay for student vouchers to private, segregated academies.

1961

In May 1961, the Commonwealth of Virginia was engaged in widespread "massive resistance" to the desegregation of public schools.

Laws had been enacted to require public schools to close rather than desegregate. A General Assembly committee, appropriately named the Committee Against the Administration of Justice, subpoenaed witnesses and their personal and business records in a futile attempt to destroy the civil rights movement in Virginia.

Massive resistance was a racist doctrine fostered by U.S. Senator Harry F. Byrd Sr. and irrationally advocated by the Richmond News Leader and the Richmond Times-Dispatch.

In the News Leader's inflammatory campaign in defiance of the Brown decision, James J. Kilpatrick occupied the now-defunct evening newspaper's traditional segregationist role as editorial page editor.

The mouthpiece for the owners of the two newspapers, Mr. Kilpatrick unsuccessfully argued that a flimsy doctrine of "interposition" gave white officials—from the state house to local courthouses—the right to resist compliance with the Brown decision that outlawed segregation in public schools.

Virginia's fierce resistance encouraged opposition to Brown across the South and delayed the ultimate acceptance of the Brown decision. The public schools in Prince Edward County shamefully closed for five-years, rather than open the doors of education to black students.

Virginia's resistance also prompted numerous public and sometimes violent demonstrations in Farmville, Danville, and many other communities across the state. State laws were enacted to divert millions of dollars of public funds to defend segregation and the system of Jim Crow. Public funds were diverted to private, segregated schools, until the federal courts condemned such practices. The Virginia State Conference of NAACP, the NAACP Legal Defense Fund, and a heroic band of attorneys led by attorneys H

Sixty years will soon have passed since the Supreme Court's May 1954 landmark Brown vs. Board of Education decision barred state-sanctioned racial segregation. Time flies. How are we doing? You may have noticed that we still have segregation, but it is not like it used to be.

Black Communities:

Jerry Walker (Dr. Mobley's great-grandfather) was one of South Boston's early master carpenters. He owned the North Main Street home pictured here, one of the most admired homes in the city. He worked with James Traver in building the covered bridge over the Dan River and later trained in carpentry under Robert R. Hamilton. Mr. Walker helped build the Planter & Merchants Bank in 1891, and was, according to the late Richard Russell Noblin Jr. the principal builder of the Noblin Home on Washington Avenue, completed in 1895. He personally shaped the timbers for the corner "doome." Mr. Walker died on June 6, 1907, while he was remodeling the Mount Vernon Baptist Church.

George Washington Ford (Dr. Mobley's grandfather) was one of South Boston's black master brick masons. See the photo of Mr. Ford and Mr. Person standing in front of the Mount Olive Baptist Church, which they bricked. Mr. Ford also bricked his son's home. See pictures.

Mrs. Arabella Walker Ford (the daughter of Jerry Walker, wife of George Washington Ford, mother of George [Dick] Francis Ford, and grandmother of Dr. Mobley) taught in a two-room school with Mrs. Kate Ragland Owen in the New Ferry/Washington City Community in Halifax County, Virginia.

Civil Rights

Although at first public law on schooling separated the races, early education was very serious in Halifax County and South Boston. The schools were located all over the county. They were built by entrepreneurs or church groups so that children in their neighborhoods could have basic education. In many of the schools, a single teacher or two taught all the classes for grades one through seven in a rustic building. There were potbelly stoves, a water bucket with gourd dippers and drinking cups, and benches. The schoolhouse was a major source of community pride, along with the post office and the church. Between hauling water from the well and chopping wood for winter, male pupils at one to four-room schools pitched in to help keep the school going, even fighting who would get the chores that day. As recitations wrapped up each morning, older students filed back to the desks, and younger student squirmed over the promise of morning recess. While pupils crowded in to the cloakroom and escaped to the yard to play, the teacher prepared for the next lesson on the blackboard. The school year was for five or six months, cut short by harvest in the fall and planting in the spring. The grade you were in was determined by what books you could get. Children passed down their books to younger siblings when they were finished with them. The thing that kept the teacher in charge of the one-room schoolhouse largely was the extension of the disciplinary role of the teacher beyond the schoolhouse door. When the rare punishment was dealt at our school, that troublemaker could count on another occurring when he or she got home. Older students escorted the younger ones to the outhouse, acted as mentors to younger classmates, and strongly encouraged self-discipline to the blending levels in one room. Despites its many challenges, having students aged five to six sitting side by side paid off in more ways than one. Most of the schools had many common characteristics. They had dirt floors, while other had oiled floor.

Mr. Alfred Breedlove and Mrs. Annie Bell Glenn Breedlove (mother of Florence Glenn Breedlove Ford and grandmother of Dr. Mobley) were prominent tobacco farm owners. In later years, after moving to the town of

South Boston, they sold the farm. While living in town, they both worked and retired in a South Boston tobacco industry.

CONCLUSION

In all too many parts of the South, blacks could not register to vote, could not serve on juries, and thus were deprived of the most basic justice.

Black children went to neglected, poverty-stricken elementary and high schools—whose schedules were often arranged so that they would not interfere with cotton picking—and could not go to the best state universities.

The indignities inflicted on blacks every day were both small and large. They could not swim in local pools, eat at local restaurants, or go to local movies theaters through the main entrance and had to sit separated from the white audience in a ghetto area upstairs.

In my memory, whenever we traveled, we had to stop along the side of the road so we could slip into the bushes to answer the call of nature. In that America, we were not allowed to use a gas-station toilet.

The Brown decision, more than any other act, political or legal, began the birth process, however belated, however slow, however difficult, and however painful, of a new America. Associate Justice Stanley Reed unanimously later said he believed it was probably the most important ruling the Court had made in its entire history.

Just sixty years earlier, the Court had upheld racism in the Plessy v. Ferguson decision (it ruled that the segregation of schools was constitutional), but now the climate was shifting. World War II, ended just nine years prior, had been fought against totalitarianism and racism. The forces that drove both Brown and, later, the civil rights movement, were in many ways the first reflection of profoundly changed attitudes among a new generation of Americans. They'd carried the burden of the war overseas and were appalled to find that some of the things they had fought against existed in their own country.

The Brown decision served as the ignition system for the civil rights movement. That movement—led by a group of young black ministers, mostly notably the Rev. Dr. Martin Luther King Jr.—gradually orchestrated a brilliant assault upon some of segregation's most toxic forms and helped turn around the conscience of the nation, watching at home on television.

HOW FAR HAVE WE COME? Some of the progress is remarkable. Not only do we have a new, ever-expanding black middle class, but also Oprah Winfrey—who could not have gone to one of the great white universities in her hometown of Nashville when she was a girl—is our most popular television host; Michael Jordan—who could not have played basketball for North Carolina before Brown—was our most popular athlete and the greatest salesman in our history before he retired; and Bill Cosby has become arguably our most popular comedian. In addition, a whole new generation of black CEOs are now leading some of our nation's most important companies.

In many ways, the educational map of the South it quite different. At the great universities of the Deep South--places where many a local politician once said that blacks would never attend—blacks not only earn degrees, they also reach new heights. A large part of the athletic programs that are the pride and joy of states such as Mississippi, Alabama, and Georgia are black dominated. Yet it also is true that, in many small towns, whites have created their own schools and have left the existing public schools—essentially still segregated—to blacks.

But there also are, and not just in the South but also in the whole country, heart-breaking reminders of both black poverty and black alienation.

Sometimes, looking back at how I and so many others felt at the time of the Brown decision sixty years ago, I think we had no sense of the extent of the damage that we, as a nation, had inflicted on black Americans in more than 200 years of intense racism, starting with the harshness of slavery and ending with the bitterness of segregation.

The legal and political change that came in during the years 1954 to 1965 was, I now think, the easy part. The hard part—in this most difficult of American journeys—is overcoming the educational, economic, and psychological damage produced over so long a period.

But that does not lessen the importance of the Brown decision as a towering historic act and the great new beginning that it represented. It allowed, to paraphrase Justice Jackson's prophetic words, the new, second America finally to be born.

We, as a nation, have made remarkable progress in sixty years. Yet the fight for true equality is far from over. New generations continue the struggle.

Betty "Liz" Ellis Ross Timeline and Other Information

1951 Betty was born in Seattle, Washington

1952 Moved to Texas

1952 Moved to Georgia

1953 Betty's brother, William Arthur was born

1954 Moved to Texas

1955 Betty's brother, Virgil Joe was born

1955 Moved to Japan

1957 Moved to Texas

1957 Betty started school in Killeen, Texas

1957 Betty's sister, Roberta Lynn was born

1960 Moved to Germany

1961 Betty's brother, Billy Ray was born

1963 Moved to Kentucky

1964 Betty's sister, Sandra Lee was born

1967 Moved to Colorado

1968 – 1970 Worked as a waitress for Prange's Coffee Shop

1969 Worked at Liberty Loan Corporation

1970 Moved to Oklahoma

1971 Worked as a GS2 at Fort Sill, OK

1972 Married Dennis C. Williams

1972 Moved to Germany

1973 Moved to Colorado

1973 Worked for Colorado Springs Equipment Company

1974 Married Blant Norris Reeves, III

1974 Moved to Maryland

1974 - 1976 Attended Harford Community College

1976 Graduated with an A.S. in Business Administration

1976 – 1978 Attended the University of West Florida

1977 Started training in martial arts

1977 Worked for Digital Systems of Florida

1978 Betty changed name to Liz

1980 Christopher Stephen Ross was born; Married Jeffery S. Ross

1981 Mark Jeffrey Ross was born

1982 Moved to Maine

1982 Started working for Ernst & Whinney

1982 Volunteered to work with the 13th Regional Corporation

1983 Moved to New Hampshire

1984 Kathryn Leigh Ross was born

1984 Became self-employed (RGMC, LLC)

1986 Kevin Michael Ross was born

1987 Started working for House of the Samurai as Program Director

1993 Registered as a Lifetime member of the All Japan Karate Do Federation

1993 Started working for the 13th Regional Corporation

1997 Graduated with a B.S. in Management

1997 Worked as a Manager with Avon Products, direct selling

1997 Started the M.B.A. program degree

1998 Graduated with an M.B.A. in Business Management

1999 Began teaching Finance at a community college

1999 Worked as an Academic Advisor (part-time) for New Hampshire College

1999 Started working on doctorate degree
2002 Started working on a grant-funded position in Florida (year 2 of a 3-year grant)
2002 Graduated with Doctorate in Business Administration in Management/Finance
2002 Moved to Florida
2002 Started teaching as an Adjunct Professor with AIUOnline University
2002 Started teaching as an Adjunct Professor with Embry-Riddle Aeronautical University
2002 Began Jewish studies after finding out grandmother Ola had Jewish roots
2003 Liz voted as Chairman of the Board of Directors for the 13th Regional Corporation
2003 Appointed Deputy Director of Fiscal and Systems Management for Florida Partnership for
School Readiness (final year of the grant)
2004 Liz started teaching as an Adjunct Professor with APUS University
2004 Liz appointed interim CEO of the 13th Regional Corporation
2005 Retired from the 13th Regional Corporation
2006 Worked for the Unalakleet Native Corporation

I spent some time in the village of Unalakleet as the General Manager for the Unalakleet Native Corporation. That was a time that I do not have fond memories; the people in the village did not want me there. My time there was the first time I had experienced severe prejudice. I was an outsider. I figured that if you are bi-racial you have no place to call home.

2006 Started teaching for the University of Alaska Fairbanks Rural Alaska Honors Institute
2006 Although not necessary, I completed the formal studies/conversion for my Jewish heritage
2010 Liz went to Vietnam to teach MBA students

Corinne Patrick, Liz Ross, Sandra Mobley

2010 Hired by the University of Alaska Fairbanks School of Management as a term instructor

2010 – 2014

Since I have been hired at the School of Management at UAF, much as happened. I was ecstatic to be hired by UAF…I bought a car and drove to Fairbanks, Alaska from Orlando, Florida during the month of December. My son Kevin, came with me since he had applied to attend UAF for engineering. During our long drive, we stopped to see my daughter, Kathryn, who was in the hospital with her first child and my first grandchild. He was born December 25 while Kevin and I were on the Alaska Marine Highway. We had quite the experience driving the AlCan Highway during December!

Although I remain the only Alaska Native in the department, it seems to be an asset rather than a detriment. I work closely with the Native Alaska Business Leaders (NABL) student organization and work on a small grant for Alaska Rural outreach and development. This has been rewarding.

Much has happened throughout my life and I would not change anything. I have learned from my mistakes and from the errors of others. I am one of 64 Alaskan Natives with a doctoral degree and the first and currently the only Alaskan Native with a Doctorate in Business Administration. I have found that some people have anti-Semitic views in some geographic areas of the U.S. and that some people have anti-Alaskan Native American/American Indian views in some geographic areas of the U.S. The values and beliefs of others I have no control. I have to withhold judgment and hope that as a country with no specific religion, culture, or ethnicity that others learn to benefit from diversity.

CORINNE PATRICK TIMELINE AND OTHER INFORMATION

1961 Corinne was born in Georgetown, Guyana.

1963 Patricia and Herb was born, Corinne's sister.

1966 Corinne stated school in Linden, Guyana.

1968 Sean was born, Corinne's brother.

1969 Deanna married Herbert Mitchell.

1970 Deanna and Herbert moved to United States with Sean and Herb.

1970 Corinne and Patricia moved to the United States

1970 Moved to Covina, California where we lived 5 years.

1972 Herbert Mitchell adopted all three of us, Corinne, Patricia and Sean, and Deanna adopted Herb.

1972 Gloria Binning, Corinne's grandmother died.

1975 Moved to Oxnard, California where we lived 2 years.

1975 Annie Mitchell is born, Corinne's younger sister.

1977 Moved to Oceanside, California where I resided until February 1981.

1981 Went into the US Army, station in Germany.

1982 Married Michael A. Patrick

1983 Kamlyn Patrick was born.

1984 Station in Germany, till 1987.

1985 Herbert Mitchell died.

1986 Manley Binning Corinne's grandfather died.

1985-1987 Attended college, received AA degree in Liberal Arts.

1987-1989 Station in Fort Hood Texas.

1987 Monica Patrick was born

1989-1992 Station in Germany.

1990-1991 Was deployed to Desert Shield/Storm

1992 Went back stateside and station at Fort Irwin, California.

1992 Miriam Patrick was born.

1994 Received Bachelor degree in Business Administration.

1994 Michael Patrick Jr. was born.

1995 Received Master degree in Public Administration.

1995 Michael Patrick Sr. retired from the US Army.

1996 Corinne was medically discharged from the Army.

1996 Michael and Corinne moved to Houston Texas.

1996 Michael started working at Memorial Herman Hospital.

1996 Corinne started working at Compaq Computers.

1997 Corinne started working at 3PL.

1999 Corinne started working on doctorate degree.

2002 Corinne graduated with doctorate degree in DPA.

2002 Corinne started teaching as Adjunct Professor at Lonestar College & AIUOnline University.

2004 Corinne left Corporate America and moved forward in teaching career with APUS University.

2006 Michael A. Patrick at age 47 after almost 25 years of marriage.

2008 Corinne started teaching at CSU.

2009 Corinne went to Vietnam teaching MBA students.

2010 Corinne went to Vietnam teaching MBA students.

2010 Angelica was born, my granddaughter, Monica's daughter.

2011 Corinne remarry to Morris Bates.

2000-2014

There have been multiple changes in my life. If I have to put a percentage on it, I would have to say 85% is good. However, I believe that the 15% is what makes us and gives us the purpose to drive forward. After the passing of Michael, I just did not think I could make it. We had a good marriage as with every marriage there are good times and challenging times. He was supportive of me being in the Army, going to school and moving forward in whatever God's desire was for us to become.

Michael was not only a soldier in the US Army but he was a soldier in the Army of God. He was a man of purpose and passion for the things of God. A man of integrity that loved his God and family. He was true to God's Word and loved God with all his heart. When he went home to be with God in December 2006, I thought my life was finish. However, God has another plan. My four children did not take it well, they loved their father and he was a true father to them. He spent time with each one and made them feel special in their own way.

In the five years before I got remarried I went through the grief process, it seems like a slow cumbersome process, however God is faithful to His Word that He is a present help in time of need and trouble. I can truly say that the Father loves me with an everlasting love and that He cares for us, even the things that men disregard.

Currently, my four children are adults and are doing well, they have adjusted to their father being gone and know they have a heavenly Father that cares for them unconditionally. Morris was chosen by God for me. As God did it the first time when He put Michael and I together, He did it again when He put Morris and I together. It is for God's purpose we live this life and it is for His purpose we surrender our lives to Him therefore He has full charge of our lives. I am forever indebted to His Son for what He has done for us "for His Grace is sufficient for us".

The Civil Rights Movement Timeline

Ten years prior to the passing of the Civil Rights Act of 1964:

1954 U.S. Supreme Court declares school segregation unconstitutional in Brown vs. the Board of Education of Topeka ruling, reversing the Plessey case.

1955 Rosa Parks refuses to move to the back of a Montgomery, Alabama, bus as required by city ordinance; a boycott follows and the bus segregation ordinance is declared unconstitutional. The Montgomery Bus Boycott started in December 1, 1955. The blacks of Montgomery decided to boycott the city buses until they could sit anywhere they wanted on the bus. When the boycott began, no one expected it would last long: however, blacks returned to the buses on December 21, 1956, over a year after the boycott began. Although the gains of the Montgomery Bus Boycott were small compared with the gains blacks would later win, the boycott was an important start to the movement, which later launched a ten-year national struggle for the Civil Rights Movement of 1964.

- ➢ Federal Interstate Commerce Commission bans segregation on interstate trains and buses.

Corinne Patrick, Liz Ross, Sandra Mobley

1956 Coalition of Southern congressmen calls for massive resistance to Supreme Court desegregation rulings.

1957 Arkansas Governor Orval Rubus uses the National Guard to block nine black students from attending a Little Rock High School. Following a court order, President Eisenhower sends in federal troops to ensure compliance.

1960 Four black college students begin sit-ins at the lunch counter of a Greensboro, North Carolina, restaurant where black patrons are not served.

> ➢ Congress approves a watered-down voting rights act after a filibuster by Southern senators.

1961 Freedom Rides begin from Washington, D.C., into Southern states.

1962 President Kennedy sends federal troops to the University of Mississippi to quell riots so that James Meredith, the school's first black student, can attend.

> ➢ The Supreme Court rules that segregation is unconstitutional in all transportation facilities.
> ➢ The Department of Defense orders full integration of military reserve units, the National Guard excluded.

1963 At sit-ins, which began on May 28, 1963, participants were sprayed with paint and had pepper thrown in their eyes. Students who sang movement songs during lunch after the bombing of NAACP field director Medgar Evers's home were beaten. Evers himself was the most visible target for violence. He was a native of Mississippi and World War II veteran who was greeted by a mob of gun-wielding whites when he attempted to register after the war in his hometown of Decatur.

According to Myrlie Evers, Medgar was a target because he was the civil rights leader. The mood of white Mississippi was that if Medgar Evans were eliminated, the problem would be solved.... At an NAACP rally on June 7, Medgar Evers told the crowd, "Freedom has never been free.... I love my children and I love my wife with all my heart. I would die, and die gladly, if that would make a better life for them." Five days later he was shot and killed as he returned home around midnight. Byron De La Beckwith, a member of the Citizens' Council, was arrested for Evers's murder, but he was set free after two trials ended in hung juries. He later ran for lieutenant governor.

- Race riots prompt modified martial law in Cambridge, Maryland.
- Dr. Martin Luther King Jr. delivers "I Have a Dream" speech to hundreds of thousands at the March on Washington.
- Church bombing in Birmingham, Alabama, leaves four young black girls dead.
- In November, President John F. Kennedy assassinated.

1964 President Johnson signs the Civil Rights Act and submits it to Congress.

- Congress passes Civil Rights Act declaring discrimination based on race illegal after seventy-five day-long filibuster.
- Three civil rights workers disappear in Mississippi after being stopped for speeding; their bodies were found buried six weeks later.
- Riots in Harlem, Philadelphia.

1965 The march started on Sunday, March 7. As marchers crossed the Edmund Pettus Bridge in Selma, named for a Confederate general, they were met by police and state troopers, some on horseback, with orders from Governor George Wallace to stop the march. The march was from Selma to Montgomery, Alabama, to demand protection for voting rights. Two civil rights workers were slain earlier in the year in Selma.

- Malcolm X assassinated.
- Riot in Watts, Los Angeles.

1966 Edward Brooke, R-Massachusetts, elected first black U.S. senator in eighty-five years.

1967 Riots in Detroit, Newark, and New Jersey.

- Thurgood Marshall is the first black to be named to the Supreme Court.
- Carl Stokes (Cleveland) and Richard G. Hatcher (Gary, Indiana) elected first black mayors of major U.S. cities.

1968 Martin Luther King Jr. assassinated in Memphis, Tennessee; James Earl Ray later convicted and sentenced to ninety-nine years in prison.

- Poor People's March on Washington--planned by King before his death--goes on.

By the end of the 1960s, membership in the Black Panthers party and the Nation of Islam had exploded. No longer did you see visions of peaceful demonstrators marching down the street singing "We Shall Overcome." The media changed its focus and began to highlight the most radical of blacks instead of those who believed in non-violence. The clean-cut, articulate spokesman, yielded to the big Afros and fiery speech of Brown, Clever, and Ron Karenga. Karenga was the inventor of the Kwanza celebration that many black Americans now celebrate. Karenga also taught in the Black Studies Department of California State University, Long Beach.

1973 Maynard Jackson (Atlanta) is the first black elected major of a major Southern U.S. city.

1975 Voting Rights Act extended.

1978 Supreme Court rules that medical school admission programs that set aside positions based on race are unconstitutional (Bakke decision).

1979 Shoot-out in Greensboro, North Carolina, leaves five anti-Klan protesters dead; twelve Klansmen are charged with murder.

1983 Martin Luther King Jr. federal holiday established.

1988 Congress passes Civil Rights Restoration Act over President Reagan's veto.

1989 Army General Colin Powell becomes first black to serve as chairman of the Joint Chiefs of Staff.

1989 L. Douglas Wilder (Virginia) becomes first black governor.

1990 President H. W. Bush vetoes a civil rights bill he says would impose quotas for employers; weaker bill passes muster in 1991.

1994 Byron De La Beckwith convicted of 1963 Medgar Evans assassination.

1995 Supreme Court rules that federal programs that use race as a categorical classification must have "compelling government interest" to do so.

1996 Supreme Court rules consideration of race in creating congressional districts is unconstitutional.

Sandra - father, George Francis Ford

Sandra - mother, Florence Glenn Breedlove Ford

Sandra - mother and I

Sandra – grandfather, George Washington Ford

Sandra – grandmother, Arabella Walker Ford

Sandra –grandparents, Alfred and Annie Bell Glenn Breedlove at their Golden Wedding Anniversary

Sandra - 1946-48 attended grades 1 and 2 at
Williams Normal and Industrial Institute

Sandra - 1948-53 attended grades 3-7 at
Washington-Coleman Elementary School

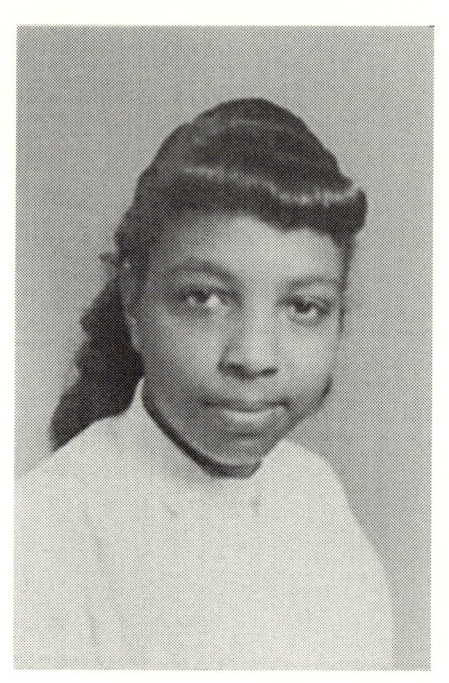

Sandra - 1953-54 attended grade 8 at Halifax County Training High School

Sandra - 1954-58 attended grade 9-12 at Mary M. Bethune High School

Sandra - 1958 attended Virginia State College for BS Degree

Sandra - brothers, George William Ford and Breedlove Ford and I attended my grandparents Alfred and Annie Bell Breedlove's Golden Wedding Anniversary

Sandra - February 1967 – My wedding day

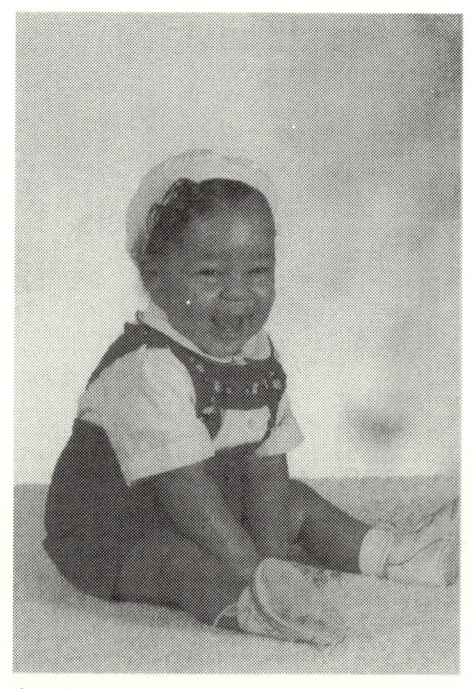

Sandra - April 1968 - son Kevin Mobley was born into this union

Sandra - 1998 receiving MBA at Averett University graduation

Sandra - 2002 receiving DPA at Nova Doctorial graduation

Sandra - 65th birthday party

Sandra – Alpha Kappa Alpha Sorority, Inc. member

Sandra – Kevin and I at Toastmasters International Induction Ceremony

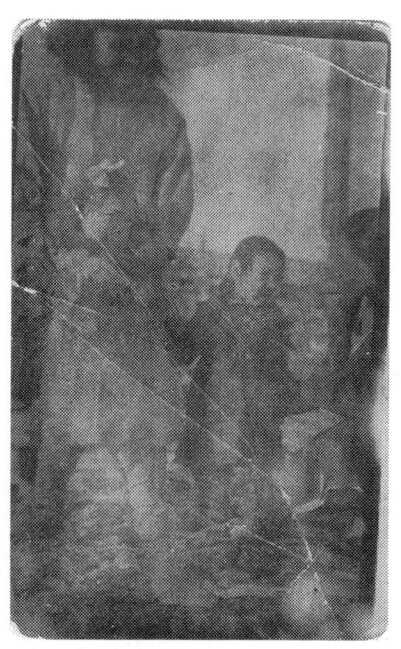

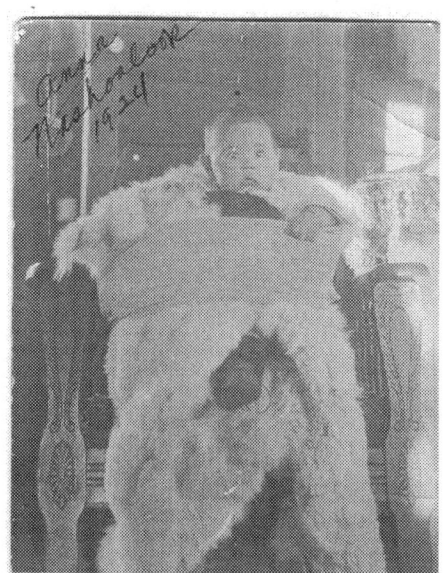

1951 Betty's mom, Anna Grace Nashoalook,
1924; taken in Noorvik, Alaska

1951 Arthur V. Ellis and Anna G. Nashoalook, 1948

Upper: Arthur V. Ellis (Betty's dad) at work, Nome, Alaska 1948;
Middle: Arthur V. Ellis downtown Nome, Alaska 1948;
Lower: Nome, Alaska 1948

Upper Left: Sister Nancy, 1949 Nome, Alaska;
Upper Right: Betty and Karin, 1952 Zapata, Texas;
Bottom: Betty, 1952 Zapata, Texas

1952 (Early Years) Chief Warrant Officer Arthur V. Ellis, Anna Grace Ellis, Karin and Betty. 1952

1952 (Early Years) Arthur V. and Anna Grace Ellis, McAllen, Texas 1952

1954 (Early Years) Betty, Mom, Art, and Karin, 1954 Zapata, Texas

Upper Left: Granny and Grandpa Ellis' home Eddy, Texas; Upper Right: Anna Ellis (standing far left) Sitting: cousin Martha, Betty, Art, Virgil, Karin and two aunts sitting to far right; Lower Left: Bottom step -Cousin Waynette, another cousin, cousin Martha Lynn, Top Step - Karin, Betty, another cousin, cousin Sandra holding sister Roberta, with brother Art holding on rail. Lower Right: Roberta in front, Virgil, Cousin Billy Ray, Art, cousin Martha Lynn, in the back is Betty and Karin

1960's Getting ready to leave for Germany, 1960. Brothers Art and Virgil in front; Karin, Betty, Roberta, and Mom Anna.

1960's Our home for four years, 4913-D Rose Terrace, Fort Knox, Kentucky

1970's Betty at Harford Community College, Bel Air, Maryland, 1975

1970's Jeffrey S. Ross & Liz, Pensacola, FL 1979

1980's-Mid-1990's Anna Grace, Aunt Mary Lou Stiles, Uncle Henry Nashalook, 1980's

Liz Ross, 3rd degree black belt with the youngest student, 1998

2002 (Nova Southeastern Years) Liz, Corinne, and Sandra, 2002

2005 Liz, sister Roberta, and sister Sandra,
2005, Colorado Springs, Colorado

2005 Liz with Suzy Villegas – 13th Regional Corporation
Shareholder Meeting, October 2005, Fairbanks, Alaska

2013 Clyde Gooden (NANA Corporation) & Liz, 2013, UAF-SOM

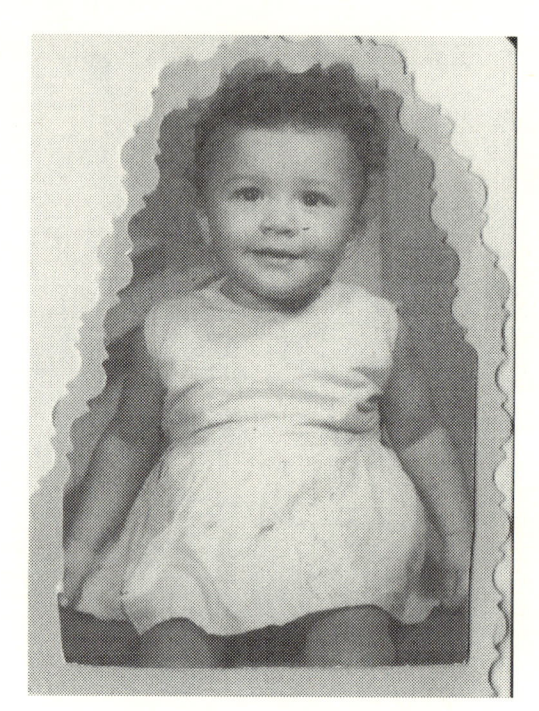

1961 Corinne baby picture

1962 Corinne and Aunt Betty

1963 Corinne and Grandfather

1960's Manly Binning

Sherry, Corinne and Grandmother, Gloria Binning

1960's Corinne and Patricia, Guyana

1970's Corinne, Sean, Herbie and Patricia family trip

1975 The Mitchell family, blended family, Dad, Mom, Corinne, Sean, Herb, Patricia, Annie and Renee (cousin)

1978 Herb and Corinne Christmas

1981 Corinne Ft. Lee Va. U.S. Army

1981 Corinne Germany U.S. Army

1982 Corinne Helibronne Germany

1982 Corinne Spain

1982 July Corinne wedding

1985 Corinne Garlstedt, Germany E-5 promotion

1988 September California, Corinne, Mom,
Kamlyn, Monica, Annie, Sis. Reed

1995 Kamlyn, Monica, Miriam and Michael Jr.

2000 Uncle Rex, Corinne, Monica, Miriam and Michael

2001 Michael and Corinne

2002 Nova doctorial graduation, Corinne,
Uncle Rex, Miriam and Michael Jr.

2002 Nova graduation, Jeff and Liz

2005 November Michael, Corinne, Kamlyn, Miriam and Michael Jr.

2005 Kamlyn and Corinne

2006 Monica and Miriam

2007 June Mom's birthday party, Corinne,
Patricia, Sean, Herb, and Annie

2009 Sean and Corinne

2011 February Morris and Corinne

2011 November Morris and Corinne wedding party

2011 November Pastor Johnson, Morris and Corinne

2011 November, Corinne, Annie, Patricia, Spencer and Miriam

2011 November "Blended Family photo"

2014 September Angelina birthday party

2013 June Michael Jr.

2014 May Morris and Corinne

APPENDIX

A Time Line Of The Civil Rights Movement	
1954 **May 17**	Landmark Supreme Court ruling <u>Brown vs. the Board of Education Topeka, Kansas.</u> "Separate but equal" schools ruled unconstitutional.
1955 **December 1**	<u>Rosa Parks</u> refuses to move to the back of a Montgomery City bus to allow a white man to have her seat, resulting in her arrest for violating the city's segregation ordinance. The Montgomery bus boycott, organized as a protest of this law, resulted in the legal challenge of the law and a victory for the boycott that lasted over a year. The ordinance was declared unconstitutional. Montgomery's buses were desegregated.
1963 **May 3-5**	A "Children's Crusade" for equality in Birmingham results in the use of fire hoses and police dogs by city police on the demonstrators, may of whom were mere children.
1963 **May 10**	The first urban riot of the 1960s occurs in Birmingham. Blacks burned white-owned property in response to another bombing.

1963 **Sept 15**	The bombing of the Sixteenth Street Baptist Church in Birmingham results in the death of four black girls.
1964 **August 28**	Two hundred thousand march in Washington, D.C. and hear the Rev. Martin Luther King Jr.'s "I Have A Dream" speech.
1965 **August 6**	The Voting Rights Act of 1965 forbids the use of literacy tests and other voter tests as prerequisites for voting. It also authorizes federal intervention to aid blacks in registering to vote in the South.
1965 **March 21-25**	Rev. King leads a five-day, fifty-four mile march from Selma to Montgomery, Alabama, for racial equality in the South.
1965-68	Urban racial rioting lasts three years in Los Angeles, Newark, Detroit, and Chicago
1968 **April 4**	The assassination of Rev. King in Memphis sets off a wave of rioting in 125 cities in twenty-nine states.
	Information for this summary came from the following: Glenn T. Eskew. But For Birmingham: The Local and National Movements in the Civil Rights Struggle. Chapel Hill: University of North Carolina Press, 1997. Flynt Wayne, et al. Alabama: The History of a Deep South State. Tuscaloosa: University of Alabama Press, 1994.

BIBLIOGRAPHY

"Jim Crow Laws" retrieved February 8, 2005 from King National Historic Site http://www.nps.gov/malu/documents/jim_crow_laws.htm

Annual Report of the Commissioner of Indian Affairs: Documents of the U.S. Indian Policy

The History of Jim Crow Website:

The Civil Rights Movement. Available at http://www.cnn.com

Civil Rights Movement 1955-1965: The Montgomery Bus Boycott." available at http://www.watson.org